Slices of a Life

PAUL GABLER

authorHOUSE®

AuthorHouse™
1663 Liberty Drive
Bloomington, IN 47403
www.authorhouse.com
Phone: 1 (800) 839-8640

Published by AuthorHouse 12/22/2015

ISBN: 978-1-5049-6065-6 (sc)
ISBN: 978-1-5049-6063-2 (hc)
ISBN: 978-1-5049-6064-9 (e)

Library of Congress Control Number: 2015918609

Print information available on the last page.

This book is printed on acid-free paper.

Contents

Preface ix
Acknowledgments xi

Chapter 1 It's the Short Game That Counts and Counts…and Counts… 1
Chapter 2 Old Cemetery Memories 5
Preamble 5
The Plot of Ground—Then 6
Old Cemetery Doings 8
Flora and Fauna 13
The "Others" 15
The Move 16
The Plot of Ground—Later 18
Chapter 3 Journeys By Thumb 21
The Early Trips 21
The Big Trip—Preliminaries 22
The Big Trip—First Day 26
The Big Trip—Second Day 27
The Big Trip—Third Day 30
The Big Trip—Notes 32
The Big Trip—Aftermath 32
Chapter 4 John Barleycorn Blues 35
Postscript 37
Chapter 5 Fathers and Sons 38
Chapter 6 The Mail Must Go Through 47
Chapter 7 Mother(s)—In Fact and In-Law 54
Chapter 8 The Little Fisherman and the Acrophobe 60
Chapter 9 Timberlane 65
Chapter 10 Three Sisters 68

Chapter 11 Entertaining the Kids 74
Chapter 12 The Silent Dog.. 79
Chapter 13 Rod and Georgia 81
Chapter 14 Begging the Question and Other Misusages 89
Chapter 15 Automotive Adventures.. 91
The 6,200-Mile Trip 91
The Cape Crusader.. 93
The Snowstorm 94
Drivers' Training.. 95
Behind Closed and Locked Doors 96
The Glasses and the Car 97
The "Oil Change" 98
Chapter 16 Travels (and Travails) in the Pacific Northwest............. 100
Logistical.. 100
Meteorological.. 102
Ecological...103
Chapter 17 Some Waterfalls I Have Known
and Other Favorite Places 105
Chapter 18 An Epitome Epiphany and Other Blind Spots 111
Chapter 19 Collaterals...113
Chapter 20 Odd Pod's Odd Jobs 121
Chapter 21 La(w) La(w) Land.. 125
Preamble 125
Wherein I Am En Route to, to wit, La(w) La(w) Land... 125
Wherein I Am Domiciled in, to wit, La(w) La(w) Land. 129
Postscript... 136
Chapter 22 Telephone Troubles 138
Chapter 23 In Memory of Beloved Manny...................................... 142
Chapter 24 More Cats and a Few Other Pets 150
Preamble 150
Heinz 150
The Cats of My First Incarnation 151
Fritzi...153
Some of Nancy's Original Cats..153
Ginger 155

The Siblings....157
The Death of Becky....158
Phoebe....160
Elmer....163
Postscript....163
Chapter 25 Meesh-i-gan!....164
Chapter 26 Classical Music....170
Chapter 27 Mr. Fun....172
Postscript....180
Chapter 28 America's Bank....181
Chapter 29 Feline Transitions and Updates....183
Chapter 30 Philosophizing....186
Chapter 31 Strange Things....190
Unexpected Destinations....190
Attraction and Repellence....191
The Speeds of Light and Sound....192
Premonitions and Dreams....193
The Moving Furniture Covers....195
Antique Antics....196
After All These Years....197
Chapter 32 The Strangest Thing....198
Chapter 33 My Redeeming Social Value....200

Appendix A Photographs....203
Appendix B On the pronunciation of the letters "ch" at the beginning of words in the English language....209
Appendix C A Tale of Two Kitties....211

Preface

I don't know that I could define a conventional autobiography, but I'm pretty sure that this book is not such. It is topical rather than sequential and concentrates on matters that I consider odd and/or amusing and/or touching.

Acknowledgments

Many thanks are owed to my wife, Nancy, and my children, Laura, Pat, Gail, Ed, and Tom, for their roles in events described in the following pages. My thanks also go to Nancy and Laura, for their work in the creation of the manuscript and for their input concerning inclusions and exclusions, and to Pat and Gail, for their efforts to preserve early drafts of many of the chapters.

Chapter 1

It's the Short Game That Counts and Counts...and Counts...

In an effort to minimize the disappointment of those who may buy this book on the assumption—based on the title—that it's a golf book, I will say a few words about my golf game. As will soon become apparent, the fewer words said about my golf game, the better.

My effort to learn the game began when I was a teenager, but I never became anything more than a mediocre golfer, at my best. A good score for me would average out to about a bogey per hole. As to a bad score—well, it wasn't quite that the sky was the limit. And I didn't quite plumb the depths reached by that legendary young man who swung and missed when teeing off at the first hole, addressed the ball again, whiffed again, and then turned to the others awaiting their turns to tee off and said, "This sure is a tough course."

What my golf game lacked was any semblance of consistency. Things would have been fine if each time I played a course I did as well on each hole as my best score ever on that hole. I don't suppose anyone ever attains that goal, but my variations were extreme. I did make good shots now and then. One time when my older brother, Rod, and I were doing some putting on a practice green, I lined up a putt aimed at a cup about fifty feet away on the other side of the green. Rod told me that he would eat his club if I made that putt, and, with this incentive, I promptly sank it. However, shots like that one, whether at the pressure-packed arena of the practice green or out on the golf course itself, were widely interspersed among a series of hacks, duffs, slices, fades, shanks, and excavations.

My long game was too short, my short game counted (in numbers that were much too high), and both my short game and my long game were misdirected. On too many occasions where the golf course layout called for players to proceed east on one fairway to one green and west on an adjacent fairway to another green, I showed that I would not be bossed around and proceeded in the opposite directions. My game had an attribute that would have been good for baseball but was lousy for golf—I hit the ball to all fields. And, of course, the objective in golf is to hit the ball on the fairway rather than to any field, for fields are out of bounds.

On one occasion, I hit a bouncing ball that struck my father-in-law, Money (his given name was Monroe), in the most fleshy portion of his body. He wasn't hurt at all—it would be a rarity for any shot of mine to have been hit hard enough to hurt anybody. And it was his own fault that he got hit. He was standing on the fairway ahead of me and off to the left instead of standing in a place of safety, directly between me and the green.

On those too infrequent occasions when I did make a good golf shot, I would often have a mixed reaction. On the one hand, I might think that I was finally getting the hang of the game, but on the other hand, I might regret wasting the good shot on the terrible round of golf that I was playing that day. An instance of such feelings occurred one day at the university course when I was in law school. I shot something like 50 for nine holes and was able to achieve this only by getting a birdie on the ninth hole. Though I didn't feel good about this episode, I'm sure I would have felt worse if I had birdied the first hole and then proceeded to shoot 50 for nine.

One good thing about golf is that a feeling it seems to engender is hope. No matter how terrible my last shot or the last hole I played or my most recent round of golf, I would frequently find myself feeling that the next shot or hole or round would be better. Almost always this would turn out not to be true, but I nevertheless continued to have such feelings.

It should be evident from what I have said that in my case, at least, the good things about golf were far outweighed by the bad. It was accordingly a very good thing that I gave up the game while I was still a young man. My abandonment of golf was probably triggered by the move out of town of the fellow sufferer with whom I most often played at the time. Whatever triggered it, my quitting the game of golf was a good result. Unfortunately, this result did not endure forever.

Some years later, I became friendly with a fellow by the name of Carl, who worked for a corporate client of the law firm where I worked, and one of the things we talked about was golf. My conversations with Carl did indeed lead to my taking up golf again after not playing at all for nineteen years.

The golf course where Carl and I first played was somewhat shorter than the usual, the par for the first nine holes being only 32. I shot 38 on this front nine, the best round of my life. However, my ecstasy was short-lived because on the back nine my score was something over 50. Thus, within a couple of hours, I had reacquired all of the bad habits and improper techniques of my golf game, which evidently had dissipated during the nineteen years of my layoff from the game.

Nevertheless, I continued to play, occasionally, with Carl or others. Carl—only partially in jest, I fear—attributed my problems on the golf course to the absence from my golf bag of two clubs which were essential to my game: a saw and a net. I suppose Carl could have added that I also lacked a third essential, a pole to enable me to vault over fences to reach the out-of-bounds areas which were the destinations of so many of my golf shots.

On one occasion I attended, as Carl's guest, the golf outing and banquet put on by a business group of which he was a member. One of the gimmicks of these festivities was that every attendee was awarded at least one prize for his achievements, good or bad, on the golf course that day, whether low gross, high net, best score on the fourth hole, worst score on the eighth hole, etc., etc. In addition, the identity of the recipient of each of the many prizes was announced during the banquet, with the recipient being entitled or required, as the case might be, to walk up to the head table and accept his award amidst the huzzahs or guffaws, as the case might be, of the assembled group. I was the "lucky" or skill-less winner of two prizes at that banquet: high gross and high net. And I won the latter award even though each player was allowed to name his own handicap and even though I selected quite a high number. Not high enough.

You would think that the mortification of being called upon to march up and receive two such prizes before a large group of mirthful diners would have caused any self-respecting human being to recognize that he was overmatched and to give up the game of golf. But not me. I pressed on to further glory or (I suppose I should say) further sorry.

I don't recall how many rounds of golf I played after the banquet fiasco, but I do recall an occasion when one of my law partners and I played nine holes with our teenage sons. I shot a little better than did my younger son, Tom, that day, my score being three strokes less than his. However, this was the first time he had ever played golf in his life!

Enough is enough. I am now (and for many years I have been) enjoying another layoff from the great game. When the subject of golf comes up in conversation now, I may be heard to say that I no longer play the game but, if I did, could play as much golf in one afternoon (strokes, not holes) as most people could play all summer. This is, of course, an exaggeration, and my sorrow is that it's not more of an exaggeration.

Chapter 2

Old Cemetery Memories

Preamble

When I was a young boy, decades ago, there was an old cemetery in Elgin, my hometown in the Chicago area. Surely there are old cemeteries in many hometowns. But this old cemetery perhaps differed from many others in that, while it no doubt originally was located at the edge of town, the city had grown so that the cemetery was surrounded by it and was located just a few blocks from the downtown business district. And my home, when I was a child, was located less than a hundred yards away from this old cemetery.

Many childhood memories of mine and, I am sure, of my contemporaries in the neighborhood are closely associated with the old cemetery, or the Old Cem, as we called it. Strangely enough, none of these memories, at least in my case, have any association or connection with ghosts, goblins, or ghouls. And this despite the fact that the Old Cem was indeed a cemetery. Although not currently in use for burials during my childhood, the Old Cem still contained many tombstones and monuments, together with the belowground objects ordinarily associated with tombstones and monuments. I have no recollection of ever experiencing a feeling of fright while in the Old Cem, either during daylight hours or after dark, by reason of the fact that the plot of ground where I found myself was a cemetery.

The Old Cem to me was not a frightening place. It was, for the most part, a wonderful, fun place, as I hope will be brought out by the following account of my memories concerning the time I spent in and around the old cemetery when I was a child.

The Plot of Ground—Then

The Old Cem was rectangular in shape and about a quarter of a mile across from north to south. From east to west, it was somewhat longer than that. The cemetery was bounded in part by city streets (including two streets that dead-ended at the southern edge of the Old Cem) and in part by the backyards and side yards of various homes.

Our house faced south and was separated from the southern edge of the Old Cem by the rear portion of the long backyard belonging to our neighbors, the Johnsons, whose house faced west. (This family included a son, called Sonny, who was a year or two older than I and who will be mentioned a few times later on.)

Much of the Old Cem was on higher ground than the areas surrounding it, and along most of the southern and western boundaries there were drop-offs, ranging from gentle to very steep slopes, of up to fifteen feet or so. As a matter of fact, there was a retaining wall, maybe four feet high, along part of the southern boundary of the cemetery at the base of the steep slope. Along its northern and eastern borders, the old cemetery was at about the same grade as the adjacent neighborhoods. However, approximately the westerly two-thirds of the northern part of the old cemetery was much lower than the portion lying to the south, so that there was a steep slope down to this hollow.

The Old Cem was crisscrossed by a multitude of pathways and trails. The main trail ran from the south edge of the Old Cem to the northwest corner. This trail served as a shortcut to downtown from parts of the city that lay south and east of the Old Cem. In those days, and especially before there was any bus service in our neighborhood, much of the travel to and from downtown was on foot or on bicycles, and this trail across the Old Cem was a much-used shortcut for many. My dad was among those who used the Old Cem as a shortcut on his way to and from his job downtown. We kids, of course, also used the Old Cem as a shortcut. For instance, Georgia (my younger sister) and I crossed the Old Cem going to and from Sunday school. Also, the Old Cem was the shortcut used by six-year-old Paul when he escorted four-year-old Georgia to nursery school at a residence located near the northeast corner of the Old Cem.

Although there was a network of other paths in addition to the main trail, don't get the idea that it was necessary to be on a path in order to go from one place to another in the Old Cem. The cemetery was a miniwilderness but by no means an impenetrable wilderness. You could pretty much go anywhere you wanted as long as you avoided running into a tree, bush, or tombstone. But just as in the case of a vacant lot or another piece of land that people walk across, trails in the Old Cem developed along the routes that most people used most often. They were created by the passage of many feet over a period of many years—there was no concrete, blacktop, or crushed stone involved.

Because the Old Cem was only an unofficial park in those days, there were virtually no "facilities" there. All that I remember is a softball diamond (including a screen behind home plate) located in the eastern part of the hollow on the north side of the Old Cem, and a monkey bar installed between two trees in the more westerly part of that hollow, which was the most heavily wooded area in the Old Cem.

Although there were no restroom facilities in the Old Cem, it was, of course, a very large outdoor bathroom for us boys. I made use of the Old Cem on numerous occasions for purposes of kidney-draining, and I'm sure that others did also. At least, I'm sure that other boys did. I was not privy (if you'll pardon the expression) to whether girls conducted similar activities in the Old Cem.

An older boy I knew of, by the name of James, clearly surpassed me in his use of the Old Cem for bathroom purposes. One day he squatted down in the weeds about fifty feet away from a group of small boys, which included me, and apparently had a movement. If I can describe my feelings at that time with words I would use now and didn't even know then, I would say that I viewed this conduct as gross—and yet macho.

It was several years after the foregoing incident that I heard the old joke where you are asked which hand you use to wipe your hind end after conducting such activities; and upon your responding either "right" or "left," the questioner happily says, "Oh, that's strange. I use toilet paper." If James had been asked such a question, I have a hunch his reply would not have been "right" or "left" but instead, "I use grass and weeds" or

"Whaddaya mean, wipe?" (My second and last wife, Nancy, who is not from my hometown, tells me that in her childhood, she was present at an incident similar to the episode which I have described. She was among those who witnessed a boy committing a moving violation in a wooded area and using some leaves to tidy up afterwards—leaves that turned out to be poison ivy. 'Nuff said.)

One other physical characteristic of the Old Cem, which I suppose could actually be considered a facility, should be mentioned. This was a neighborhood dump, a very common feature of towns in those benighted times. This particular dump was located in a hollow at the south edge of the Old Cem, a short distance east of the Johnsons' backyard, and was accessible by car from the easterly of the two streets dead-ending at the Old Cem. The dump wasn't very large, maybe thirty yards from east to west and fifteen yards across. And, of course, the ground on all sides of the dump sloped down into the dump.

I am sorry to say that for me there was an unfortunate connection between the dump and the use of the Old Cem as a hangout, so to speak. One evening, after dark, Sonny and I stood side by side at the top of the slope on the edge of the dump, with the intention of relieving ourselves into the dump. I accomplished this function soon—and before Sonny had even begun. For some unaccountable reason (call me stupid, and you'd be right), I then walked in front of Sonny, and just at that moment, he got it going. Not only that, but, because of the slope, my head was at the same level as Sonny's peeing apparatus as I passed in front of him. I got out of the line of fire quickly but was there long enough for my hair to get a dousing. (I'm glad to say that Sonny didn't give me an earful, as well.) The next stop, presumably after Sonny completed his function, was the stationary tub in the Johnsons' basement, where Sonny and I washed... and washed...and washed my hair.

Old Cemetery Doings

Although at the start I referred to the Old Cem as a wonderful, fun place, the only incident involving me that I have described so far was certainly not fun and, in fact, was a real pisser. However, that dump-side episode could be regarded as wonderful—in the sense of curious and strange.

Most of the time, though, the Old Cem was indeed fun and wonderful. Wonderful in the sense of great. It was wonderful for the kids in our neighborhood to have such a big, wild place where we could roam around and play. The neighborhood boys played a lot of "guns": sometimes cowboys versus Indians, sometimes cops versus robbers, but most often just we'uns versus you'uns. The cemetery was an apt setting for gun battles involving cowboys, for it would well qualify as a stand-in for Tombstone. Toy guns only, of course, in these encounters—although a stone-throwing battle was not unheard of. We also did some tree climbing, played with dogs or watched dogs fight, and played holly, kick-the-can, red light, etc. And I recall that Sonny and I sometimes used areas in the Old Cem near our homes as battlegrounds for our toy soldiers.

The Old Cem was also a scene of friendly or not-so-friendly wrestling matches from time to time. For that purpose, the Old Cem had an advantage over other areas because it was a much larger grassy area than the yards and tree banks in the neighborhood. And the larger the area of grass where you are wrestling, the less likely you are to face the biggest danger in a neighborhood wrestling match—namely, the discovery, after it's over, that while rolling around on the ground, you had come into contact with dog shit.

Much of the time we boys just wandered around the Old Cem to see what was going on and to look for something to do. We weren't looking to do anything bad—we weren't vandals. However, we did swear. I recall that when I was about five years old, it was my belief that the group of boys of which I was a part had invented the word "shit." Though this possibly is not the case, we definitely used the word and, at least in my case, without sufficient self-restraint. I refer to an incident that occurred when I was about eight and my classmates Jack and Jim came over to my house. We decided to go upstairs to play, and my sister decided to come along with us. I decided to make it a race and proclaimed that the last one upstairs would be "a ball of shit." When three eight-year-old boys and one six-year-old girl race upstairs, you know who's going to finish last. I announced the result in the following terms: "Georgia's a ball of shit." Georgia relayed my announcement to our mother, who announced that Jack and Jim should go home. And then my mother introduced me to the taste of soap.

On one occasion, when I was up in the Old Cem with several other guys, we noticed that one of the houses in the neighborhood was on fire. As has been the custom with boys forever, we hightailed it down to that house to watch the firemen fight the fire. It happened that a fireman on the roof had an accident with his ax and cut his leg pretty bad. I remember feeling faint when I saw the fireman's leg bleeding onto the roof. This was the first time I became aware of being squeamish about the sight of other people's blood, though I have never felt that way concerning my own blood.

When I was a small boy, my contemporaries and I played ball, usually bound-out-work-up or some other informal game, at the ball diamond I described earlier. However, we would more often play ball in the Johnsons' big backyard at the edge of the Old Cem. On these occasions we also spent time in the Old Cem, looking in the tall grass and weeds for a thrown or batted ball that had ended up there.

Once in a while we played touch football in the old cemetery, though there were very few flat areas suitable for football. The ball diamond wasn't a good spot for football because too much of the surface was bare dirt. I remember playing touch football with three other neighborhood kids, Fred, Dick, and Pat, in a flat area at the foot of the slope right along the west boundary of the Old Cem. Pat was kind of a tomboy at the time and could keep up with us boys. Years later I heard that she and Fred had married. Maybe he played a different style of touch football than I did.

Naturally, my contemporaries and I didn't play only in the old cemetery. We also played in the Johnsons' backyard, as I've mentioned, and elsewhere in the neighborhood. One game that, as far as I remember, we never played in the Old Cem and played only indoors was strip poker (not coed). I particularly recall one game at Bill's home, involving Bill and Ward (both of whom were a little older than I) and me. At one stage of the game, Ward was close to naked, and Bill and I were fully clothed and each in possession of some of Ward's clothes. Right about then, we heard Bill's mother start the process of unlocking the front door of the apartment upon her return from shopping or whatever. This prompted some very fast action by several young boys, as Bill tried to get Ward and me out the back door before Bill's mother discovered what we had been playing and what condition Ward was in. The departure process was, of course, much more of a problem for Ward than for me, but we were able to make our escape.

The older boys had organized softball games at the ball diamond in the Old Cem, including games between teams from different elementary schools during the school year. Also, for a period of years, there was a summertime softball league consisting of teams representing a number of playgrounds in the town, one of which was the Old Cem. One of the players on the elementary school and playground teams was my brother, Rod, who was seven years older than I. Rod, being left-handed, usually played first base. During the time when Rod played on these teams, and during a number of years thereafter, I must have watched dozens and dozens of softball games at the Old Cem. By the time I became old enough to be a player (but not much of a player), the playground league had been disbanded, and, as best I can remember, grade school games were no longer played at the Old Cem. Or maybe I don't remember playing in a grade school softball game at the Old Cem because I wasn't good enough to be on the team.

An unusual feature of the ball diamond in the Old Cem was the rather steep upward slopes in center field. At the top of the first slope of perhaps four feet, there was a rather narrow flat area. Beyond that was the second and steeper slope, the top of which must have been about twenty feet higher up. As I said earlier, the ball diamond was indeed down in a hollow. So, playing center field at the Old Cem could be quite a dangerous adventure. If you didn't keep your eye on a fly ball, you wouldn't catch it. If you did keep your eye on the ball, you might fall and break your neck!

Luckily, most of the time the center fielder could stand at the foot of the first slope because it was rather unusual for anyone to hit a ball even as far as the top of that slope. However, I remember one occasion when a ball was hit much farther, during a softball game between two grade school teams. There was a real slugger on the team that was our school's opponent that day. When he came to bat, our center fielder was signaled by his teammates to back way up—and in view of the layout of this ball diamond, when a center fielder moved back, he did indeed also move up. In this instance, the center fielder did not move far enough back *or* far enough up. The slugger hit a home run that, as I recall, landed about halfway up the second slope and bounced the rest of the way up the hill.

Things got completely turned around at the ball diamond during the wintertime. The sledding began at the top of the second slope, and the destination was the pitcher's mound or home plate or the screen behind home plate. The ball diamond area was the center of sledding activities because the other lengthy slopes in the old cemetery had plenty of trees at the bottom and on the way down.

And sleds were the wintertime vehicle of choice at the Old Cem—I don't recall seeing any toboggans or skis. Some sled substitutes were also used, like garbage can lids and shovels. Shovels had an advantage over lids in that the handle could be used to steer to a certain extent, and you didn't have to rely only on leaning your body. There was at least one way in which sleds were different in those days—the runners ended in a point at the back instead of curving up and connecting with the rest of the sled frame. I remember this particularly because one of the times when my sled and I took a tumble while going down the hill, I got poked, just above my eye, by one runner of the sled. A close call but no real harm done, though I still have a small scar.

My brother was a very impressive figure to me when I was a young boy. (This remains true even now, when I am an old boy and Rod has sadly passed away.) Once, when Rod was probably about fourteen years old, he deigned to give me and a few of my contemporaries a chance to wrestle with him, all at once. As you can imagine, he had no trouble with us, and seven-year-olds were soon being tossed all over the place.

Sometimes my activities in the old cemetery did not involve any of my contemporaries but consisted of my tagging along after Rod and his gang of older boys (using the word "gang" in the sense in which it was applied to boys in those days). I don't recall any specific incident involving Rod's gang that occurred while I was present; what I do recall is my feeling of pleasure at being allowed to be with or near those older boys on any occasion.

It may be that I had kind of a mascot status with Rod's gang. I've seen one snapshot of him and several of his friends grouped around this one beaming little boy (me). Also, Rod's pals had a couple of nicknames for me: Little Taters and Bugs Jr. These were derived from Rod's nickname of Tater Bugs, which in turn was derived I know not whence. (I say "potayto"; you say "potahto"; they said "tater.")

Flora and Fauna

Although the Old Cem was not actually a forest, various types of trees, both coniferous and deciduous, were scattered through it. Some areas, particularly the deep hollow near the northwest corner and the area along the northern border, were quite heavily wooded.

In addition to trees, assorted bushes, grasses, wildflowers, and other plants grew there. The most prominent bushes were the lilacs, great clusters of which were located near the southwest and southeast corners of the Old Cem. Also, there was a large cluster of lilac bushes at the top of the hill overlooking the ball diamond. Some of these lilac bush clusters must have been at least twenty feet long and ten feet across. The lilacs were, of course, beautiful in the spring when in bloom. After the bushes leafed out, they became useful as a hideout, a fort, or some other kind of outpost in the games we played.

Long grasses were involved in a spectacle we boys enjoyed observing at the Old Cem from time to time, when the local fire department burned areas of long grass and weeds. We didn't know, or even think about, the reason these fires were started—we just liked to watch the fires. I suppose that the fire department's purpose was to burn off dry grasses and weeds in a controlled fire in order to reduce the possibility of someone else accidentally starting a larger, and uncontrolled, fire.

Probably the most important to me of the plants found in the old cemetery was asparagus. On many a spring or early summer morning, I would awaken, or be awakened, very early to go up into the old cemetery to hunt for and pick wild asparagus—which involved, incidentally, getting my clothes soggy from the dew that seemed to cover bushes, grasses, and everything else. Because I conducted many expeditions for asparagus, I got to know numerous locations where the asparagus grew. However, there was always a chance of stumbling onto some choice asparagus at a spot previously unknown to me.

Locating the asparagus was only one part of the exercise. An equally important part was arriving at a decision as to whether to pick the asparagus I had located. Sometimes the decision was easy. Of course I would immediately pick any stalks of asparagus that had reached optimum size and maturity. But what about those stalks that were not very far out of the ground yet and would be far more desirable to my mother if allowed to grow for another day or another few days? The decision is still easy, you say? Why not just come back in a day or in a few days and then pick that asparagus, you say? I'll tell you why not: the competition.

There were other hunters and pickers of asparagus working the same territory as I was, and it seemed to me that most of them were old ladies wearing shawls or kerchiefs on their heads. Like me, they became aware of the spots in the Old Cem where the asparagus grew. The existence of competing asparagus pickers was, of course, the reason for getting up into the Old Cem as early as possible in the morning. When I caught sight of one of those old ladies in the Old Cem, I sometimes had the impression that she and I were in a race to reach one or another patch of choice asparagus. And when I located some asparagus, I was often faced with the dilemma I mentioned earlier—where picking now would mean picking nonoptimal asparagus but coming back to pick on another day might mean that one of those old ladies would pick this asparagus in the meantime. Or even Georgia might do so. She did some asparagus picking too, and I sure wouldn't want my little sister to beat me out of some good asparagus!

Another thing, besides asparagus, that could be picked up in the Old Cem was grass snakes. These snakes were, of course, harmless, but it seemed to be an exciting event for us boys to happen upon a grass snake during the course of our games or roaming. Naturally it was a terrifying event for the snake to be surrounded by a group of boys, possibly poked with sticks, and possibly picked up by one or more of the boys. I don't believe we did any harm to a grass snake, except perhaps to its psyche. And I don't recall whether I was one of the boys who picked up grass snakes. I've never been big on snakes.

Other animals also made their homes in the old cemetery: rabbits, squirrels, various types of birds, and, in the dump, rats. I remember one occasion when we were saddened to find that our cat, Tuffy, had wiped out a nest full of baby rabbits.

As far as I can recall, I never saw a raccoon or an opossum and never saw or otherwise became aware of a skunk in the Old Cem. My impression is that these types of animals are more common within cities nowadays than they were many years ago. For example, on the evening I took Nancy to Elgin for the first time, we saw a skunk walking along a sidewalk in a residential neighborhood.

The "Others"

Looking back, I think that I had something of a proprietary feeling about the Old Cem: a feeling that the Old Cem somehow belonged to the people who lived along its south edge, a feeling that it was our Old Cem. Nevertheless, I was not disturbed by the fact that on certain occasions, such as good sledding days in the wintertime and school or playground league softball games, there were many people in the old cemetery who were strangers to me.

At other times, when I observed boys and girls who were unknown to me playing in or wandering around the Old Cem, I had a reaction that I can best put into words as, "Who are these other people and what are they doing in my old cemetery?" I think I had a similar reaction regarding my old lady competitors in the wild asparagus business. Most of these "Others"—children or adults—probably lived in other neighborhoods adjacent to or near the old cemetery and, regardless of where they lived, obviously had as much right as I did to be there. I'm describing my memory of my reaction to the Others and certainly don't seek to justify my feeling.

One particularly unhappy episode involving Others sticks in my memory. The Others were a grade school classmate of mine, Billy, and two or three of his friends. Billy lived about half a mile away from the Old Cem. I don't believe I had ever seen him in the Old Cem prior to this episode, but I had always regarded him as a friend. Perhaps he didn't feel so friendly toward me because, on a prior occasion, I had disrupted his birthday party by getting into a fight with another guest.

In any event, what happed on the day in question was that, within one of those big clusters of lilac bushes in the Old Cem, Billy and his friends pantsed me. For the benefit of those who are uninformed, the verb "pants" is of the same type as the verbs "skin" and "scalp"; one who is pantsed is actually de-pantsed, at least temporarily.

So what's so bad about getting pantsed? After the perps depart, why not just put on your pants and go about your business? I think the problem has to do with concepts of dignity and honor, which I believe are important to a child, even if not thought of in terms of those words. When the indignity of being pantsed was inflicted on me, I believe what I felt was a sense of having been dishonored. In any event, after this incident there was no question of friendship between Billy and me.

The Move

When I was twelve years old, our family moved away from our home near the south edge of the old cemetery. We didn't move very far away in terms of distance—our new home was a couple of blocks north of the Old Cem. I think it was a more dramatic move from a psychological standpoint, partly because I liked our old house so much. Obviously it was the only home I had known, but it also had some features that appealed to me. I liked the fruit cellar at the foot of the basement stairs, with its nooks and crannies among the shelves and under the stairs.

Also, at the front of the house, there was an attic setup, which I had always considered interesting and, in a way, mysterious. In a corner of each of the two front bedrooms, there was access to a small attic area that could be walked into but was transformed into a crawl space by the sloping roof as you proceeded toward the front of the house. In addition, there was a crawl space all along the very front of the house connecting the two attic areas. One of the front bedrooms was the room that Rod and I occupied during much of my childhood, and the other was our parents' bedroom. I rarely, if ever, went into the attic area of my parents' room, but from time to time I would go down to the end of our attic area and look across the connecting crawl space as if I were gazing for the first time on previously unexplored territory.

For me, the trauma of the family's move also had to do with the Old Cem. I now attended a different grade school, and some of the children who were now in school with me and who lived in my new neighborhood were children I had previously seen in the Old Cem and had regarded as Others. After our family's move, it almost seemed to me that I had become one of the Others, and I didn't spend near as much time in the Old Cem as I had previously. In actuality the main reasons for this were no doubt nonpsychological. My contemporaries and I were getting older, and because of the geographic move, I didn't hang around nearly as much with the boys in my old neighborhood with whom I had played in the Old Cem. I spent most of my time now with new friends in my new neighborhood, new friends who did not spend as much time in the Old Cem as I had been accustomed to do. Our cat perhaps had more trouble than I did about becoming one of the Others. Not long after we moved, Tuffy ran away and never returned.

One regular connection I had with the Old Cem after the move involved my mowing the Joneses' lawn. They lived a block south of the old Cem on the street that served as the cemetery's west boundary. The Joneses' son, Bill, was a friend of mine, but he didn't mow the lawn because his parents didn't have a lawn mower. The one we had was an old contraption with steel wheels, no rubber tires. The thing I remember most vividly about my lawn-mowing job was the rattle and clatter made by this old lawn mower as I rolled it along the sidewalk from our new house to the Joneses' home, including all the way along the west side of the old cemetery.

About a year after we moved to our new home—on Halloween night, as I recall—someone threw a rock through an upstairs bedroom window at the Johnsons' house. This was a particularly serious matter because pieces of the broken window glass fell into the crib in which the baby daughter of Sonny's older sister slept, though I believe she was not in the crib at the time. The culprit had evidently thrown the rock from the Old Cem, which was about twenty feet away from the Johnsons' house and was on the same level as the upstairs window by reason of the steep slope at the edge of this part of the Old Cem.

There was a police investigation of this rock-throwing incident, and evidently the Johnsons gave my name to the police as someone who might have committed the crime. Whether I was the only suspect or one of a long list I never learned. That I was a suspect became known to me a short time after the incident when I was called out of my eighth-grade class and summoned to the school principal's office, where I was questioned by a police officer. I truthfully assured him that I had had nothing to do with the rock-throwing incident and knew nothing about it.

A police interrogation of a thirteen-year-old boy, with no parent present and without any prior notice to the boy's parents, is something that apparently could happen in a bygone era. As far as I know, my parents never learned, from me or anyone else, of this visit to the principal's office.

(I should acknowledge that, during my grade school years, I had other command performances in the principal's office. But I am writing about the Old Cem here, and none of the other visits had anything to do with the Old Cem.)

The rock-throwing incident and its aftermath seemed to have no effect on my relationship with Sonny. I continued to see him now and then (though, of course, not as often as when I lived next door to him), and we never discussed the incident. One of the things we did was shoot baskets in his backyard, where a backboard and rim were attached to a tree and where the playing surface was either dirt or, if it started to rain, dirt turning into mud. So I was willing to play basketball with a kid who had pissed on my head and whose parents had evidently suspected me of criminal conduct. I suppose one reason for my willingness was Sonny's possession of a basketball and backboard and my possession of neither.

As concerns Sonny's parents, I don't believe I ever exchanged a word with either of them after the rock-throwing incident, not that we had had frequent conversations previously. On their behalf let it be said that, although they suspected me of criminal conduct and had only my word that I was innocent, they never sought to bar me from their backyard.

The Plot of Ground—Later

At some point in time, years after the events I have described, the city fathers decided to convert the old cemetery into an official park. This involved a variety of steps and took quite some time, especially because these steps included the removal of tombstones, monuments, and all remaining remains.

There was also a great deal of grading work done, which significantly changed the topography of the Old Cem. The dump was, of course, done away with, as were virtually all of the trails and paths. The southern half of the Old Cem is now pretty much flat all the way across, although there is still a drop-off along the south edge and a slope along the west edge. The northerly part of the Old Cem is still much lower ground, and a grade school was built in the hollow at the northwest corner. Also, tennis courts were installed to the east of this school.

In addition to the removal of trees necessitated by the construction of the school and installation of tennis courts, virtually all of the trees and bushes were removed from the southerly portion of the Old Cem. However, a closely planted row of small trees was placed along much of its southern edge. As a result, it is now necessary to peer between leaves and branches in order to see our former home from the Old Cem.

Because I continued to live in the Chicago area, I have been back to the Old Cem several times during my adult years. Because of the passage of time and the changes in topography and flora, I have had the feeling, each time I have returned to the Old Cem, that I was now a stranger in my own land. And I didn't like my own land nearly as much as formerly. That part of the Old Cem which is closest to my old home could be described (as of the most recent time when I was there) as flat, bare, barren, and desolate.

The topographical changes in the southern part of the Old Cem and the stripping of trees and bushes from this area made it a much better setting for informal football games than it had previously been, and my two sons and I made use of it for that purpose a couple of times when we visited my hometown during their youth. We had our own variety of a three-man touch football game, which involved one defender facing two offensive players and the latter being required to announce, before each play, whether it would be a run or a pass. Well, it worked for us!

My brother and sister lived on the West Coast for many years and, naturally, didn't make it back to our hometown nearly as often as I have. I remember one occasion when Georgia and I revisited the Old Cem as adults and noticed a teenage boy standing in the yard in back of our childhood home. Georgia, who has always been much more of a go-getter than I, suggested that we find out if we could go inside our former home and led the way over to the boy, explained who we were, and wangled an invitation to take a tour of the house. The house, of course, did not seem as spacious as when I had last seen it twenty years earlier.

I believe that Rod was back at the Old Cem just once during the many years that he lived on the West Coast, and my wife, Nancy, and I were with him then. While we were there, Rod walked off by himself and stood for quite some time, lost in thought, looking down at the area where the old softball diamond had been.

The scene was reminiscent of the Indian summer drawing that appeared in the *Chicago Tribune* every autumn for years, showing an old man and his grandson looking at a number of corn shocks and showing the corn shocks being transformed, in their eyes, into a group of Indians dancing around a campfire. Nancy and I each had the reaction that Rod was looking at the softball diamond area and was seeing a ball game being played by those boys, himself included, who had played there so many years ago. As I had formerly watched Rod play ball, I was now watching Rod muse about the days when he played ball.

Our wonderful Old Cem was gone—but not forgotten.

Chapter 3

Journeys By Thumb

The Early Trips

During my teen years, I did quite a lot of hitchhiking. Nowadays, people believe that hitchhiking is a much more difficult proposition than it was at that earlier time. However, at the time I took up hitchhiking, it was common knowledge that it was a lot tougher to hitchhike than it had been years earlier during the Great Depression.

At any rate, my first hitchhiking venture consisted of a trip to a town about fifty miles away to see a football game between our high school and theirs. I went with Bill Jones, who, you may remember, was the son of some folks who, at least during an earlier period of time, didn't own a lawn mower and consequently hired me to mow their lawn.

Bill and I made it to our destination, located the high school stadium, and watched the game. I don't remember who won, but it was, of course, dark night by the time the game was over. I also don't remember whether Bill and I had discussed, or even thought about, how we would get back home after the game. We probably figured that we would mooch a ride with some other kids from our town who had driven a car up to the game; but I know we had not lined up a ride with anybody in particular. We were, in fact, lucky enough to get a ride home from somebody or other. I think this episode exemplifies one of what I'll call the principles of hitchhiking: "In the case of round trips, hitchhikers generally are much more thorough in planning the trip out than the trip back."

My next hitchhiking of any distance occurred about a year later, when I was sixteen. This was a trip to Champaign-Urbana, about 150 miles south of where I lived, to visit my cousin Virginia, her husband (who was in school there at the University of Illinois), and their baby daughter. My route down to Champaign-Urbana was along a state highway that ran straight north and south about fifty miles west of Chicago but didn't connect any major towns. So, it was slow going, with a series of short rides. But it was pleasant to be out in the fresh air and sunshine on a nice autumn day.

This trip served as a good demonstration of another principle of hitchhiking: "Hitchhiking is a good way to learn that patience is a virtue and that there are times when that virtue must be practiced." No matter how much you stamp your foot and loudly demand that the next car stop and pick you up, it won't happen unless the driver decides to do so—or unless you happen to be a woman with legs such as Claudette Colbert displayed in *It Happened One Night*.

On my return trip from Champaign-Urbana a day or two later, I took a different route, along a U.S. highway running toward Chicago. I thought there would be more traffic on this road and, thus, more frequent rides. Unfortunately, I got kind of a late start and my progress was not as swift as I had hoped. I made it home that day but not until well after dark and after it had started to rain. Would you believe that another well-established principle of hitchhiking runs as follows: "Hitchhiking at night is much more difficult, and hitchhiking at night in the rain is absolutely dreadful."

The Big Trip—Preliminaries

During the months following my Champaign-Urbana trip, I talked with Don, a high school friend of mine, about hitchhiking to California the next summer. I had an interest in going to California because several close relatives on my mother's side and also Dick, one of the boys I had hung around with in the Old Cem, had moved to southern California within the last few years. My conversations with Don gradually developed from a pipe dream about hitchhiking to California to a definite intention to make such a journey, but then things were cut short when a parental decision put the kibosh on Don's participation in the trip. (As it turned out,

Don and I were also college classmates and did, on a couple of occasions in later years, hitchhike together en route home from our East Coast university.)

Don's inability to obtain parental consent led to my planning to make the California trip alone. A departure date was set, and I went to bed the night before with the intention of setting out the next morning. That same night my parents went to a bridge party with a number of other couples, and my plans were apparently a major topic of discussion. The folly of these plans (particularly, as I gathered later, the idea of hitchhiking through the mountains) was evidently impressed upon my parents by their friends, for upon returning home my parents awakened me and advised that they had decided that I should forego my planned solo hitchhiking venture.

My parents were nice about it, said they were sorry to disappoint me, and suggested that perhaps I could go out to California by bus with my cousin Patty, who was four years older than I and was making such a trip in a couple of weeks to return to the Los Angeles area, where she then lived. My memory is that I was not at all devastated by my parents' decision. I suspect that I had some misgivings of my own about hitchhiking some 2,200 miles by myself. And the prospect of getting to California in another way that summer also helped. I expect that most people, then and now, would think that neither hitchhiking nor taking a bus from Chicago to Los Angeles is a prospect that is at all appealing.

In any event, the bus trip did soon occur, and Patty and I, as always, got along fine. The west was all new to me because, prior to this time, I had never even crossed the Mississippi River. The bus followed the northern route toward the West Coast and then turned south through Utah to Nevada. I remember when we stopped in Las Vegas, I put a few coins in a slot machine at the Golden Nugget, which was near the bus station downtown. I also recall passing by the Flamingo Hotel, standing all by itself on the outskirts of town.

Most of the time while I was in southern California, I stayed with my aunt Mary and her husband in La Cañada, but I also stayed some days and nights at Dick's home in Los Angeles. I went around some with Patty, visited another aunt and cousin who lived in Temple City, another L.A. suburb, and hung around with Dick and some of his friends.

Dick and his friends smoked, so naturally I took up the habit. They also introduced me to a somewhat different method of hitchhiking, which we sometimes used in getting around the area. What we did was approach a car stopped for a red light and ask the driver, for instance, "Are you going to Santa Monica?" Unless the driver denied any such intention, our next step was to hop into the car. Sometimes this worked.

Another thing that happened to me for the first time while I was with Dick and his friends was that I became aware of someone having an encounter with a gay man. One of Dick's friends used the bathroom at a restaurant near Hollywood and Vine and, upon rejoining the rest of us, said that he had been accosted by a man in the bathroom. At this point, I'll express my belief that one reason for whatever homophobia exists in some straight males of my generation (not that there's anything right with that and not that I feel such a phobia myself, as far as I know) is that the first contact many such straights had with gay persons was as recipients of unwelcome advances by gay men. Also, and obviously, one reason why such encounters occurred was that in those days, it was more difficult for gay men to meet others of the same orientation.

At some time during July of that summer, I took another bus trip, from Los Angeles to Phoenix, to visit my mother's younger brother Howard and his wife, Bonnie, who lived in the little town of Mesa, just east of Phoenix. At that time, Uncle Howard had just bought or leased a gasoline station out in the desert between Mesa and Chandler (an even smaller town, south of Mesa) and was about to start operating the station. I helped him in this, and we each worked ten to twelve hours a day for the next ten days or so.

One of my more unusual chores at Howard's gas station was to get rid of any black widow spiders I came across. One morning I found one under the front of the toilet seat in the men's bathroom. Fortunately, I ran into this spider in the course of inspecting the bathroom rather than in the course of sitting on the toilet. Yipe! Speaking of Arizona desert fauna, I found it interesting that the animals I generally noticed scurrying around the area were lizards rather than the squirrels I was used to in the Midwest.

After dark the lights under the canopy of the gas station were the only lights for some distance around and seemed to attract a large percentage of the insects that inhabited Maricopa County. It almost seemed that you couldn't walk through the area under the canopy because it was solid insects from the ground up. (I recognize that now there are many more lights and other man-made objects, as well as people, in the area that used to lie between Mesa and Chandler.)

One morning after I had worked at the gas station for about ten days, Howard and I got into an argument about something or other, and the upshot was a mutual agreement that our working relationship should end. Accordingly, I stalked across the station driveway toward the road, stuck out my thumb, and got a ride into Mesa in the first car that came along. You might know that I had my best luck ever at hitchhiking just at the wrong time. If I had stood by the road for a while without getting a ride, both of us might have cooled off and resolved our disagreement. As it was, the decision that I would no longer work at the gas station became fixed and, as I recall, a day or two later I took a bus back to L.A. Obviously, I wasn't going to work at Howard's gas station forever, and perhaps we both felt that this was as good a time as any to move on. I believe Howard and I parted on good terms. We remained on good terms thereafter, although, for geographical reasons, we saw one another only rarely.

How long I remained in southern California after returning from Mesa I don't remember. I do know that by then my mother had arrived by train to visit her relatives in the L.A. area. I believe we both stayed for a while at my aunt's home in La Cañada. But it was time for me to think about going home, and I still had the hitchhiking bug. Negotiations on the subject with my mother eventually produced the following agreement: If I would take a bus through the mountains—that is, to Albuquerque—I could hitchhike the rest of the way home.

In early August, I got on a bus one more time and headed east. The most memorable part of this bus trip was coming down the mountain through Jerome, Arizona, at night. Jerome is an old mining town, the main street of which winds down the mountainside in such fashion that, repeatedly, a vehicle traveling down the street (and I do mean down) is almost directly above another part of the street where it will be a few moments later.

In any event, late the next morning I got off the bus in Albuquerque on a beautiful sunny day, ready to begin what I am calling the Big Trip. This trip was destined to reinforce most of the principles of hitchhiking which I have already mentioned and also to demonstrate a couple more: (1)

"Sometimes it is better to hitchhike through a big city, and sometimes it is better to hitchhike around it—and God only knows how to decide which is the better route in any particular case." (2) "Although automobile drivers may be in danger from hitchhikers, hitchhikers may also be in danger from drivers—and other hitchhikers."

The Big Trip—First Day

My destination, Chicago, was now about 1,300 miles straight ahead of me on U.S. Route 66. Also straight ahead of me, despite my mother's intentions, were the Sandia Mountains. However, the mountains proved to be no problem at all, for one or two rides brought me, by about two o'clock that afternoon, to a place called Clines Corners, a highway junction on the other side of the mountains. As I recall, Clines Corners consisted of a gas station, a restaurant, and cars and trucks whizzing by from time to time at high rates of speed. Clines Corners was to be my world for the next six hours.

As is evident from what I just said, the hitchhiking was no good at all at Clines Corners. After I had been there for some time, I don't recall how long, I was joined by another eastbound hitchhiker, who was dropped off there, as I had been earlier, by a driver who was turning either north or south at the junction. This fellow hitchhiker was perhaps a little older than I and was heading for Tucumcari, about 100 miles east. As he soon displayed to me, he had a wooden leg, which had a little door or panel in it that gave him access to the knives he kept inside the wooden leg. Prostheses were different in those days.

Naturally, the chance of any driver stopping at Clines Corners was further reduced by there now being two of us standing there soliciting an eastbound ride. Although I was the first to arrive at Clines Corners and would have preferred to hitchhike alone, I saw no practicable way to induce my companion to relocate his operations to a point somewhat farther east, especially after he had shown me his knives. Also, it wouldn't be very sporting to ask a man with a wooden leg to take a walk.

Many minutes and many vehicles passed while the two of us stood there with our thumbs out. And then there were three. Late in the afternoon, we were joined by a kid about my age who said he was from Boston, had violated some kind of probation by leaving there, and was westbound. I am wondering now, and perhaps you are too, how two eastbound hitchhikers and one westbound hitchhiker would happen to be standing together and talking. My memory is hazy, but it could be we were standing on a median. In any event, as night approached, the conversation took a somewhat unpleasant turn, with my two colleagues talking about possibly disposing of me before the night was over. I think they were joshing me...I think.

At some point in the evening, we decided to try a variation of the hitchhiking method that I had seen used by my friend Dick and his friends in Los Angeles. We went into the restaurant at Clines Corners and approached diners at their tables with an inquiry as to whether they had room for any additional passenger(s). We were desperate, and we, or at least I, got lucky. Two fellows in their twenties who were heading for South Carolina said they would give one of us a ride for a while. I was elected because I had the longest eastbound trip ahead of me.

So, at about eight o'clock, I finally departed from Clines Corners. At some point thereafter, my two benefactors decided that I might as well stay with them until they turned off Route 66 at Oklahoma City, which was sure all right with me. Most of the time spent by them in driving to Oklahoma City was spent by me in sleeping. Bright and early the next morning, I was dropped off at the western outskirts of Oklahoma City, because it was thought that I would be better off taking the bypass around the city than hitchhiking right through town.

My six-hour stay at Clines Corners, the longest time I ever waited for a ride in my life, had been followed by the longest single ride I ever had, some 450 miles. Such is the nature of the beast that is hitchhiking.

The Big Trip—Second Day

If the bypass was the better way to go by Oklahoma City, hitchhiking through town must have been absolutely horrible. It seemed to take me forever to get around Oklahoma City and back onto Route 66. The bypass took me through the little country town of Edmond (which I understand is not nearly so little any more), and I stopped and had breakfast there.

This is as good a place as any to talk briefly about economic matters. I remember virtually nothing about my meals on this trip, but I know

I didn't eat often or much. I believe my total expenditures between Albuquerque and Chicago were somewhere between three and five dollars, and I probably had only about another five dollars in my pocket.

After getting past Oklahoma City, I spent the rest of the day, which was a Saturday, getting across the rest of the state by means of a series of short rides, of which I have no particular memory, and some walking. As night came on, I was at a diner in a little town near the northeast corner of the state. After having something to eat, I stood outside, put my thumb to work, and got a ride that I remember *very* well.

Almost as soon as I got in the car, the driver told me that it's hell when your wife is pregnant. I said nothing or, perhaps, "Um…uh." He went on to say that he was going to another town up the road to see a lady friend and get laid. My contribution to the conversation was as before. Then he said that this lady would take on anybody as long as his dick was big enough. Next, before I knew it, he reached over and took ahold of my manhood and said that he thought I would be acceptable to his lady friend.

My memory is that the driver did indeed indicate that I would not give the woman short shrift, so to speak, though this may be a case of wishful recollection. However, let me hasten to add, my thoughts at the time were not running in terms of, "Oh, boy, I qualify to get laid by this nymphomaniac," but rather in terms of, "Holy shit, this guy just grabbed my dick."

While I was still in shock from what had occurred, the driver said that he suddenly remembered that he had forgotten his rubbers (which is what condoms were usually called in those days), that he would have to return home to get them, that he would drop me off where he had picked me up, and that he would pick me up again if I had not gotten another ride before he returned. I, talkative soul that I am, said nothing or, perhaps, "Um… uh." In any event, I was soon back at the diner.

I'm sure I don't recall all of the thoughts racing through my mind at that time. I don't recall whether I wondered why he would keep rubbers at home where his wife might find them or why he wouldn't just stop at a drugstore and buy some more rubbers. I don't recall whether I considered the possibility that his rubbers story was just a dodge and that his actual intention was to get together with some friends of his and then pick me up again and cast me in a different role in the evening's festivities. What I do recall is that I had a fixed determination not to get back into a car driven by a man who had just put his hand on my gennies or some part thereof.

The only way I saw of carrying out my determination was to suspend my hitchhiking efforts for a sufficient length of time. If I stayed in the diner instead of standing at the curb with my thumb in the air, I could avoid any chance of this guy stopping to pick me up again. I probably stayed in that diner for an hour or two and then, with some misgivings, went back to hitchhiking.

Pretty soon I got a ride from a fellow who was going to Joplin, Missouri, which was about fifteen miles up the road. The driver was a heavyset man who drove with his left hand on the steering wheel and his right hand on the seat beside him. (Bear in mind that in those days automobile seats were of the bench type rather than bucket seats.) In view of my recent experience, I was very anxious about that right hand on the seat—and what it might possibly do. I'm sure I watched that right hand out of the corner of my eye for the entire fifteen miles, and I expect that I was doing some trembling as well. But the right hand didn't move, and I arrived safely at Joplin, by which time it was pretty late at night.

From Joplin I got another ride, which I believe took me to a country crossroads near the little town of Webb City. By now the cars on the road were few and far between, and I didn't really have any alternative but to continue trudging along the road in the darkness. My miseries increased when I accidentally stepped into a ditch beside the road and got shoes, socks, and feet wet.

Then I met another hitchhiker walking along the shoulder of the road. If I wondered what on earth a hitchhiker was doing out in the middle of nowhere at that time of night, he may have wondered the same thing. In any event, we walked on together along the road. It didn't seem appropriate to tell him that I would prefer to walk alone, especially because he was bigger and stronger than I was (most everybody was—and is). I mentioned to this guy that I had fallen into a ditch, and he said that I should avoid doing that because that's where the rattlesnakes are. Now he tells me!

After a time we came to a junkyard, which I believe was on the outskirts of Webb City, and decided that we should try to sleep sitting up in the cab of an abandoned truck we noticed there. If you regard me as an idiot for spending the night in the cab of a truck in a junkyard with a man

I had just met, particularly in view of what had happened to me earlier that evening, my response is that I had no feasible alternative. Besides, if this guy had wanted to rob me or assault me, he could already have done so.

But could I fall asleep under these circumstances, or would I spend a terror-filled night watching my companion out of the corner of my eye? My last day as a sixteen-year-old had been a very long, very tough day, and it turned out that I had no trouble at all falling asleep and sleeping soundly through the night.

The Big Trip—Third Day

In the morning, the two of us started walking along the road and soon came upon yet another hitchhiker going in the same direction. Inasmuch as I was the youngest and least unsavory looking of the group, we decided that the two of them would walk on ahead, and if I obtained a ride, I was to ask the driver to stop and pick up my two friends who would be a short distance up the road. I don't remember how many times this system worked, but I know it got the three of us at least one ride.

This ride took us to Springfield, Missouri, and was with a fellow who did not seem to be a particularly careful driver. At one point, while we were going along on two-lane Route 66 at a rather high speed, he wanted to tie his shoe or pick his nose or something and asked me to take the wheel. (Being the first hitchhiker he had picked up, I was, of course, in the front seat.) I managed to steer during the brief period that the driver was otherwise occupied, and we managed to reach Springfield.

When the three of us disembarked, my colleagues were unhappy with me for landing a ride with a drunk driver. It was a strange time to be drunk (more likely, hung over), and if I was supposed to know that he was drunk, why didn't they figure it out and decline the ride? Regardless of the merits of the case, the other two decided that we should change our system, that I should walk on ahead for a ways, and that if they were able to get a ride they would ask the driver to pick me up. At the time we were at the foot of a very long slope on the outskirts of Springfield, and I set out to walk the half mile or so to the top of this slope. I never saw my fellow hitchhikers again.

I must have stood at the top of that hill for an hour or two. Over and over again I would see a car start up from the bottom of the slope, would tell myself that this was the car that was going to stop for me, and would see it whiz by my outstretched thumb. Finally, though, I got a ride with a man who was going all the way to St. Louis, somewhat more than 200 miles ahead. So, once again, a long wait was followed by a long ride.

By the time we were approaching St. Louis, it was very late in the afternoon, and the driver gave me two options: He could let me off at the outskirts so that I could take the bypass around the city, or he could drop me off right downtown. In view of all the time it had taken me to get around Oklahoma City on the bypass the day before, I decided that I would prefer to be dropped off downtown. Bad decision. Downtown St. Louis on a Sunday evening was a terrible place for hitching a ride.

The details of the rides (and walking) that it took to get me across the river and into Illinois have departed from my memory and become lodged in my forgettory, but I do know that quite a bit of meandering was involved. Ultimately, I got back on Route 66 in Illinois, headed north toward the next Springfield, and it was dark again.

At the end of one ride I was let off at a highway junction south of Springfield where a road coming from the east joins Route 66. As I stood at this corner, a bus came along the road from the east and stopped in front of me. The bus door swung open and the bus driver looked out at me. I told him I was hitchhiking and he told me to hop on. Sweet man! I stood at the front of the bus near the driver as we headed for Springfield, the destination of the bus. He suggested that I would have better luck taking the bypass around town and accordingly let me off where the Route 66 bypass began at the south edge of the city.

As far as I can remember, it only took one ride for me to get around Springfield, with a guy who was probably about ten years older than I. This was another of those memorable rides. Everything was okay until he pulled off the road because, as he said, he had a piss hard-on and needed to take a leak. Although I felt uneasy hearing that kind of talk, our journey resumed without incident. However, when he stopped the car at the north edge of town, he asked whether I wanted to get together that night. I told him no, but he went on to ask whether I felt like getting a hard-on. Again I said no, and then I got out of the car and got the hell away from there.

I didn't like being accosted verbally, but at least it wasn't as traumatic as being accosted physically.

Luckily, it didn't take long for me to get a ride in a truck that took me all the way from Springfield to Chicago, about 200 miles. I slept most of the way, and it was daylight when I was let off at an intersection on the west side of the city. I believe I took some form of public transportation downtown, and then I completed my travels by taking a train home to Elgin.

The Big Trip—Notes

1. Up to now, similar to most tales, either fictional or nonfictional, I have not covered the subject of my bathroom-type activities during the Big Trip. In this connection, I will tell you that I did not emulate James, my acquaintance from earlier old cemetery days, and that I sometimes did make use of gas station bathrooms. The rest of the time I was scared shitless.
2. The name of the Oklahoma town where I was picked up by the guy with a pregnant wife was Commerce. A number of years later I learned that Commerce was the hometown of a contemporary of mine, Mickey Mantle.
3. My travels during my lifetime have been confined to the contiguous forty-eight states and three Canadian provinces. At the time of the Big Trip, U.S. Route 66 passed through the far southeast corner of Kansas, and the only time I have ever been in that state was during the short ride, referred to above, from Commerce, Oklahoma, to Joplin, Missouri.

The Big Trip—Aftermath

The trip I have been describing gave me my fill of hitchhiking for a while, and it was all of three weeks before I hit the road again. This time I hitchhiked to Cincinnati to visit my old friend Bill Jones, whose family had recently moved there. I spent about a week there and then got a ride back home with Bill's older sister's boyfriend, who had been down to visit her.

The hitchhiking to Cincinnati was uneventful, thank God. I covered most of the distance in one ride in a truck that picked me up somewhere between Lafayette, Indiana, and Indianapolis and took me all the way to Cincinnati. I want to mention one incident that points up the difference between trucking now and trucking prior to the freeway era. Indianapolis seemed to be full of railroad viaducts, and my driver apparently had a truck that was higher than most and, thus, had a hell of a time finding a route through Indianapolis because of the difficulty of finding viaducts the truck could clear. It seemed like whenever we got through a viaduct there would soon be another one on that street which was too low, and we would need to detour to another street to see if we could clear the viaduct there. Et cetera. All in all, we took a rather roundabout route through Indianapolis.

Please don't get the idea, from my description of my activities during that summer, that I was a kid who had never worked a day in his life. That summer was the exception rather than the rule. Previously I had worked about a year and a half as a Western Union bicycle messenger. When I was back in school after that summer, for my last semester of high school, I also had a job as a restaurant busboy. And after I graduated from high school in January of the next year, I worked at several jobs during the period before I started college the following September.

The first of these jobs was working in a gas station for my uncle Bob, another of my mother's younger brothers. This station was located in the Chicago suburb of Oak Park, and I hitchhiked there in the morning and took the electric railway line home at night. My uncle could take me to the railway station at night after we closed the gas station, but he couldn't pick me up in the morning because he had to open the gas station. Hence the hitchhiking. This job lasted only two days before I decided that hitchhiking in February in the Midwest was not for me.

One other incident is part of the aftermath of my so-called Big Trip—a conversation I had with a high school classmate by the name of Steve at a beer party during the Christmas–New Year holidays following my hitchhiking summer. Steve and I had known each other since we started in Sunday school together when we were about three years old. However, we had not always gotten along with one another and were acquaintances rather than friends. At any rate, the conversation I refer to went something like this:

Steve: "Hey, Gabler, were you hitchhiking down in Oklahoma last summer?"
Paul: "Yeah."
Steve: "I thought that was you."
Paul: "Oh?"
Steve: "My dad and I didn't have room in the car anyway."
Paul: "Oh."

Chapter 4

John Barleycorn Blues

As I just mentioned, the conversation with a high school classmate by the name of Steve took place at a beer party. And it was indeed during the autumn following my hitchhiking summer that I began drinking beer. Thereafter, though I have never been what I would consider a heavy drinker, the consumption of alcoholic beverages was associated with a lot of good times and also with things that were not so good. An example of the latter was my performance at the party hosted by the parents of my first wife, Barbara, to announce her engagement to me, on which occasion I managed to drink myself into unconsciousness.

Although I don't want to bore you with a parade of descriptions of additional drunken escapades, I will describe one incident that evolved from something I did when drunk because it demonstrates, at least for me, some of the workings of guilt and regret and because, just possibly, it may strike a chord with you. The incident in question is certainly not the only instance where I have mistreated another person or persons and for which I feel regret, but it is the only one I will describe here.

During our college years, I arranged with a friend of mine, by the name of Mort, to go on a double date to a formal dance during the Christmas break. Mort had previously informed me and some of our other drinking buddies of some private information relating to his girlfriend, information she had asked him not to disclose to anyone. On a later occasion (but prior to the day of the dance), when I had had a lot of beer to drink, I blurted out this private information in the presence of Mort's girlfriend, and as a result she broke her date with him. When I learned of this a day or two later, I called my date, Marlene, and broke our date.

And why did I break my date with Marlene? Because I was not much into dancing, had never been to a formal dance, and didn't feel like going to this dance without Mort being along for support. Big deal. I didn't feel like it!

There may be some sentiment that I'm making a molehill out of an anthill. After all, people break dates all the time (though a formal dance is rather a significant date). It may occur to you that it's likely Marlene doesn't even remember the incident—or me. Or if the incident is—or I am—lodged in the unconscious storehouse of her memory, it may be that no thought of either will ever occur to her conscious mind unless evoked by some Proustian trigger.

But all that is just the point. Although Marlene may not remember, or never think about, the incident or me, I have often remembered and thought about the incident and her—with regret that I could treat anyone with such callousness and indifference as I displayed. I recognize that all the guilt and regret I have felt over the years cannot even begin to undo the pain I inflicted upon her at the time I broke our date. I expect to continue to feel this guilt and regret until the day I die—and, perhaps, thereafter.

It may be said that, if breaking that date with Marlene was the worst thing I ever did, I hardly rank among the major villains of history. But please understand that my intention is not to create a catalog of my bad acts and to determine the ranking of this episode among them. Such a catalog is more of a project than I care to undertake. My objective here was only to describe what happened with Marlene and how it has haunted me ever since. She may have forgotten me, but I haven't forgiven me.

The idea that the injured party is the one less likely to remember such an incident tends to be confirmed by an entry that, a few months after the foregoing episode, I made in a half-assed journal in which I made notes on a very intermittent basis during my college years. This entry reads in part as follows: "Remember this shaft!…Repayment for [Marlene]? It is not so nice when you are on the receiving end, is it?" I have failed to follow my own directive—I don't remember that shaft or who shafted me. I assume some young lady dumped on me, but I have utterly no memory as to who was involved or what happened. I hope that whoever it was is not haunted by the incident like I have been haunted by my mistreatment of Marlene.

To return briefly, and in a lighter vein, to the more general subject of the consumption of alcoholic beverages, I want to mention that when I was quite young there was a signal (if only I could have recognized it) that I should think twice about getting involved with drinking. The first time I ever tasted beer I was about ten years old and was accompanying my uncle Howard, and caddying for him, while he played a round of golf with some other men. Afterwards we stopped at the nineteenth hole at the clubhouse, where the men had some beer and Howard let me have a sip of his beer. Looking back now, I can see that I should have been more wary about something with which I first had contact at a golf course.

Postscript

I have not consumed any alcoholic beverages (not one sip) for more than ten years.

Chapter 5

Fathers and Sons

My dad died of a heart attack during my sophomore year in college, when I was nineteen. His death occurred on a Saturday, during the college's week-long spring break, which I spent at the home of a classmate; I didn't learn of his death until I returned to my room at school on Sunday evening. There I found a message to call home, a telegram advising me of his death, and a letter from him dated three days earlier. My dad's death was quite a thunderbolt; I had no idea that there was any problem with his heart. Perhaps he had no idea either. Any warning signs may have gone unrecognized. As we all know, there's been a lot more publicity in recent years about early warning signs of heart trouble and about what should be done when such signs make an appearance.

When I read my dad's last letter, I don't believe I had any sense of it being like a communication from the other side. During those first hours—and while I was a thousand miles away from the scene—I had difficulty grasping the fact of his death. One of the things he mentioned in the letter was that he was looking forward to making a visit to my brother and his family and to seeing the "walking doll," Rod's sixteen-month-old daughter, Linda, who was the only grandchild that my father ever saw.

It probably happens often, in a case where a relative or friend dies, that we not only feel the loss but also feel regret that we said or did something we shouldn't have or failed to say or do something we should have, in our relationship with that person. One of my regrets with respect to my father was that too much of our limited time together in the last couple years of his life, during which I was away at college most of the time, was spent in negotiation or argument about two things: my use of the family car and my drinking, and about the dangers of a linkage between those two things.

Years later, when my sons were teenagers, I learned that the older boy, Ed, sometimes spent time in the parking lot drinking beer with coworkers after finishing work at McDonald's. I told Ed that I wanted him to stop doing that, and his response was that I had drunk beer when I was a teenager. (I wonder who the bigmouth was who told him that.) In any event, I then said to Ed that just because my father had let me get away with teenage beer drinking didn't mean I was going to let him get away with it. Ed stopped the drinking immediately (as far as I know) and has now been a teetotaler for a long time.

Whenever I feel the least temptation to pat myself on the back because of the foregoing incident, I need to remind myself that my father didn't "let" me get away with teenage drinking and that I continued despite his efforts to get me to stop. The difference in the two teenage drinking situations was not in the way things were handled by the fathers but in the way the sons reacted. I had a better son than my father did.

During the last fourteen years of his life, my dad worked in the local post office. He didn't even finish high school but was a capable guy and worked his way up to be head of the money order department. He was also very handy around the house and during my childhood always seemed to be fixing or working on something or other. Among other things, he did a lot of canning—I remember rhubarb, applesauce, and bread-and-butter pickles.

A couple other things he worked on that I remember very well were Christmas gifts for me. One, which I found under the tree one Christmas morning, was a wooden fort he made for my toy soldiers. The other was a beautifully finished wooden box, with a hinged cover, in which I could keep my childhood treasures. Gifts like these helped make Christmas the second-best day of the year. (The best day, of course, was the last day of school before the start of summer vacation.)

I still have the box that my dad made for me, and it still contains "treasures" from earlier eras of my life. This exemplifies something that I expect is common with a lot of people: Once you store something away—in an envelope, a carton, a box, or whatever—it may remain where it is stored for years, or even decades, without any thought being given as to how long the stored item should be retained. Once it's stored, it's *stored.*

My father had one special project I would hear about sometimes when I asked him where he was headed and he responded that he was going up to sweep the sunshine off the roof. I helped him out about as much as most boys helped their fathers, I think, but I didn't participate in the sunshine sweeping.

My dad was able to whistle in a very loud and shrill manner, and during my preteen years his whistling was the usual means of letting me know when it was time to come home. It seemed that wherever I was, in the neighborhood or the old cemetery, I could hear that whistle; my recollection is that I was quite good at promptly responding to my dad's summons.

In my early teen years, I spent a lot of time at the desk in my bedroom doing high school homework or reading. My desk sat right in front of a window, and I may have spent more time in gazing absentmindedly out the window than in the other activities. Once in a while I would be at my desk on a day when my dad was washing the upstairs windows, and I would be sure to stay where I was until he appeared at my window. His appearance there would not come as a surprise, for I could hear the ladder first being placed at my window. Nevertheless, I always got a kick out of seeing him suddenly appear just on the other side of the glass. I think he also got a kick out of the situation.

Probably my father's largest project was the home on Watres Place, where he and my mother and Rod lived before Georgia and I were born. Although I'm not sure of the details, I believe my dad played a major role in the design and construction of that house.

On December 7, 1941, I was the first one in the family to hear about the attack on Pearl Harbor. While the rest of the family was getting ready for Sunday dinner or otherwise occupied, I was up in the room I shared with Rod, listening to the Bears-Cardinals football game. The game broadcast was interrupted with news of the attack, and of course the news was transmitted by me to the rest of the family within moments.

During the war years my dad had a victory garden, and I think I accompanied him and helped out almost every time he went to do gardening. As an adult, I have done my share of gardening and yard work, but I am nowhere near the handyman that my dad was. That trait apparently skipped a generation, for Ed is more like my father in the handyman department. However, Ed evidently appropriated most of the supply of handyman abilities available to his generation in the family, for my younger son, Tom, tells me that he is more like me in that respect.

Back when I was a kid, there were some things that made Sunday an especially good day. After coming home from Sunday school, Georgia and I would rush over to the Schultzes' house, next door to ours, where they always had the comics section from a Chicago paper ready for us to pick up. In the years before Georgia and I learned how to read, Dad would read the comics to us. We would sit on his lap and follow the wooden pointer that he moved from panel to panel as he read.

Then on Sunday evenings Dad would pop some corn and all of us would sit and eat the popcorn while we listened to the Jack Benny radio program. This tradition continued for years, even to the time when I was a Western Union messenger during a couple of my mid-teen years. On Sundays my Western Union schedule was a strange one, from noon to two and then four to six. Because the show started at six, I would hustle home on my bike as fast as I could in order to hear as much of Jack Benny as possible.

Throughout my childhood and youth, my dad gave me haircuts. He also took advantage of these occasions to give me what he considered fatherly advice and what I considered lectures. Sometimes he would tap me on the head with the scissors, as a means of regaining my attention and stressing some particular point. During the early years, he also used hand clippers in his barbering. Sometimes I would get pinched on the neck by these clippers. I'm sure this was inadvertent on his part, rather than a means of emphasizing a really important point in the lecture. But I'm also sure you can see that, for more than one reason, I thought his later acquisition of electric clippers was a big step forward.

Sometimes, when we encountered one another, my father would greet me with some such salutation as the following: "Hi there, old pill, pal, Paul, old boy, old sock, old stick-in-the-mud." However, his objective when giving advice at haircutting time was to steer me away from being a stick-in-the-mud, or a bump on a log, or a cow's tail. (As an aside, I'll remind you that I've already mentioned that Georgia has always been much more of a go-getter than I. So, although I feel sure that he didn't realize it at the time, my dad was in effect telling me to be more like my little sister. Yipe!)

It would be possible for me to argue that my father was unjust in accusing me of having cow's tail, etc., tendencies. I could point out that when I was in Boy Scouts, I reached the rank of Second Class. If you reminded me that Second Class is quite a low rank in scouting, I would try another tack and exemplify my leadership qualities by calling your attention to the fact that, in my freshman year in high school, I lost an election for student council representative by just one vote. If you responded by pointing out that I would have won the election had I not voted for the opposing candidate, I guess you would have me cornered, and I would have to acknowledge my cow's tail, etc., tendencies.

Although I remember the major subjects on which my father advised me while cutting my hair, by no means did I hang on his every word. I had other things to do during the haircut and therefore could not always pay close attention to what my dad was saying. For example, I needed to examine all of the objects that were visible to me from where I sat on a high stool in the basement, where the barbering took place. Even today I can remember the model name of our coal-burning furnace: Floral City Queen. I also needed to watch the shadows that raced back and forth on the basement walls as my father, in moving around me as he cut my hair, again and again bumped into the bare lightbulb hanging down on a cord and set it to swinging back and forth—and back and forth. I fear I was more nearly hypnotized by the dancing shadows than by my father's words of wisdom.

My dad's barbering activities were not confined to me. I'm sure he cut Rod's hair as well, although I have no specific recollection of being present on any occasion when this occurred. Of course, watching someone else get a haircut ranks right up there with watching paint dry, so it's not surprising that I would be elsewhere at such times. Also, I may have felt that if I were present on such occasions, I could possibly become the recipient of the lecture even though someone else was the recipient of the haircut.

One person who I particularly remember as having his hair cut by my dad was Uncle Bob. Bob would come over to our house now and then, and, after he and my dad had chatted for a while, it seemed to me that, almost invariably, my dad would ask him whether he would like a haircut and Bob would reach up, feel his hair, and say that he guessed he could probably stand a haircut. I believe I came to the conclusion (rightly or wrongly) at some point that Bob's purpose in coming for visits was to mooch free haircuts. Whenever he came over he seemed to be pretty shaggy, and, when my dad raised the subject of a haircut, Bob reacted with seeming surprise, as if a haircut had been the furthest thing from his mind. I wondered why Dad would always volunteer to give this guy a haircut. Perhaps he figured that Bob was ultimately going to maneuver him into a haircut and that he might as well save time and get right to it. On the other hand, my dad may have focused on being nice to Bob, without concerning himself as to whether Bob was being nice to him. Come to think of it, that's a pretty good approach to things.

As far as I know, my dad's barbering activities did not include giving shaves but, unfortunately for me, he used a straight razor to shave himself. I say unfortunately because his use of a straight razor meant that he had a razor strop, and the razor strop was his instrument of choice when his younger son misbehaved to such extent as to be in need of a spanking. On those rare (ha!) occasions where I failed to do what I was told or failed to do it fast enough, my dad sometimes inquired as to whether it would be necessary for him to stand over me with a club. Any verbal response I gave at such times would express my view that such activity would not be necessary, but I knew that if he stood over me with anything, it would in all probability be the razor strop, not a club.

In addition to "old pill, pal, Paul," etc., another appellation my father had for me when I was a young boy was Beelzebub. At that time I thought this was a funny name my dad had thought up. Later, of course, I learned who Beelzebub is supposed to be. However, I don't recall now whether there was any particular connection between my dad's use of the Beelzebub terminology and his application of the razor strop.

My father, like my mother, had several brothers, and the one to whom he was closest was Joe. Whenever he called Joe's home on the telephone, the first thing he said was, "I was told to call this number and ask for Joe." When I was a little boy I thought this was a strange way to begin a telephone conversation, but I was at that time unaware of the Prohibition-era derivation of a telephonic salutation of that kind.

Both Joe and my dad played chess, and under my dad's tutelage, I took up the game at a young age. For quite a few years, he and I played chess often, and sometimes Joe would come over, and the three of us would take turns. At first, I was, of course, very much inferior to my dad and Joe in chess-playing ability, but I caught up gradually and believe that ultimately, I pretty much held my own with each of them.

When my dad and I played chess in later years, he would give his undivided attention to the game, whereas I would often carry on a conversation with my mom, who was usually sitting in the same room reading a magazine or darning socks or doing something else. On some occasions when I was waiting for my dad to decide on his next move, I would go out to the kitchen and then come back to the chess board with several slices of that great delicacy, peanut butter bread, arranged on my hand and part of the way up my arm. Sometimes I got the impression that my dad was a little frustrated that I could compete with him although I didn't always pay as close attention to the game as he did.

Inasmuch as my dad and Uncle Joe were the only persons with whom I played chess prior to entering college and because I had pretty good success against them, I got the idea that I wasn't too bad a chess player. At college I received a rude awakening when I played a kid from Brooklyn in the lounge at the freshman dining hall. He annihilated me and made it pretty clear that he felt nothing but contempt for my feeble chess-playing efforts. I believe this instance was the only time I played chess at college.

In my adult years, I taught my older son how to play chess (to the extent that I was able to teach something at which I was only mediocre myself), but Ed and I played very seldom in comparison to all the time my dad and I had spent playing the game. As a father, Ed carried on the tradition by teaching all three of his daughters how to play chess.

My sons and I were involved together from time to time in various types of sporting activities. I've already mentioned our touch football games and the single, and much-lamented, occasion on which I played golf with my younger son. The three of us played basketball on the driveway from time to time, and it seemed that Ed and I would frequently bump heads. This didn't happen with Tom and it may be that, being a couple of years younger than Ed, his head didn't often get as close to mine as Ed's did. On one occasion when I was trying to scoop up the basketball on the run, I scooped too low and tore off a fingernail. This, of course, hurt like hell but, surprisingly, not as bad as I thought it would.

During another driveway basketball game, while I was dribbling (the ball, that is) toward the basket, I felt a severe pain in the back of my right calf and went down in a heap. That ended my basketball for the day, and a few days later I headed for an orthopedist, where I learned that I had ruptured my plantaris muscle (at least that's my memory of what the doctor called it), that it could be surgically reattached, and that it was not uncommon for people in my situation to get along without an attached plantaris muscle. I have done so ever since.

Ed started jogging with me (and a friend of mine also named Ed) when he was very young. Tom did so as well, but not as regularly as Ed. They both turned out to be good runners. I believe Ed set a record for his junior high school in the mile run. Both of them were on the track and cross country teams in high school although Ed had to give up competitive sports after a year or two because of various ailments, including knee and leg problems.

When Tom was a young boy, he was virtually unique, I think, in his ability to entertain himself with imaginary sports events in which he would play all of the roles. For example, in the case of baseball, he would stand at the place in our yard that he had selected as the pitching mound and then wind up and pretend to throw a pitch, all the while describing aloud, in his role as television broadcaster, just what the pitcher was doing. Then Tom would go to home plate, take off the baseball cap he had worn as the pitcher, put on a different team's cap, pick up a bat, and get ready to hit the imaginary pitch. Again, as the television broadcaster, Tom would describe where each imaginary pitch was thrown, ball or strike, and what, if anything the batter did with each pitch. If the batter got a hit, then Tom would become the base runner, and I expect there were instances where Tom ultimately threw himself out at home plate.

During this time an older couple lived next door, and the husband (as he often acknowledged to me) spent a good deal of time looking out his window in utter fascination, watching this little boy playing a baseball game and describing it for the "television audience," all by himself. I recently learned that Tom was not as near-unique as I had thought, for

I have been advised that his youngest son, Micah, has emulated Tom in presenting one-man baseball games for the "television audience."

Both of my sons were sports fans, and here again Tom was unusual, in that, for a boy who lived in the Chicago area, he had a strange assortment of favorite teams: the New York Knicks, the New York Rangers, the Baltimore Orioles, and the Dallas Cowboys. And he was loyal to these teams and followed them closely. On one vacation the boys, their mother, and I (at Tom's request) took an off-season tour of the stadium near Dallas where the Cowboys played their home games. The stadium was at the junction of two freeways and was, of course, easy to spot. However, it seemed to me that the signage was unclear and that it was therefore difficult to reach the stadium—difficult to determine which ramp to take to exit the freeway and difficult to determine what turns to make once off the freeway. I decided that it's much easier to reach a stadium in unfamiliar territory on game day, when all you need to do is follow the stream of cars ahead of you.

On a prior vacation with the whole family at Ocean City, Maryland, we drove in to Baltimore one day to see a game between the Orioles and the White Sox. Because the rest of us were Cubs fans, seeing this game was not a big deal for us—but it was a thrill for Tom, especially when the Orioles won. That day was particularly harrowing for me because I had strained my neck (badly enough to see a doctor and get some muscle relaxant) while trying to do a little body surfing a day or two earlier. On the day of the baseball game, I still felt pain in my neck every time I turned my head. Under those circumstances, driving a round trip of some 250 miles was quite unpleasant; but I'm glad we did it.

Chapter 6

The Mail Must Go Through

While he was employed at the post office, my dad once told me a story that exemplified how important it was for the mail to go through. He said that if a police car, a fire truck, an ambulance, and a mail truck all reached an intersection at the same time, the mail truck would have the right of way. Years later when I was driving a mail truck in the course of delivering parcel post, I had occasion to test the doctrine my dad had expressed. I arrived at an intersection at the same time as a passenger car driven by John Q. Public and naturally assumed that I had the right of way. However, John Q. did not stop, so at the last instant I had to come to a screeching halt. (Perhaps the rule to which my dad had referred applied only to police cars, fire trucks, and ambulances and not to ordinary passenger cars.)

My screeching halt in this instance created a special problem because of the design of mail trucks in those days—namely, there was only a driver's seat in the front and there was a large opening between the front and back so that the driver could get a parcel from the back of the truck when he made a delivery, without getting out and going around to open the back door. However, by reason of these features of the truck design, my screeching halt resulted in a lot of my parcel post becoming airborne and flying through that big opening from the back end of the truck up to the front. In a sense, some of that parcel post was converted, for the moment, into air mail.

During my late teen years and for a few years in my early twenties, I worked at the post office on a number of occasions, either in Elgin or, while I was in law school, in Ann Arbor, Michigan. I had a variety of assignments during these years, and the following description of my activities will relate to the way things were done then. I know virtually nothing about current-day post office operations and practices, though I recognize that, particularly in the handling of mail within a post office building, things are very much computerized, automated, etc. Perhaps the design of mail trucks has also changed.

During my last year in law school, I drove a mail truck around town to pick up outgoing mail from various mailboxes. Naturally, I had a specified route and a specified schedule, the objective being to pick up mail from each box at or about the time listed on that mailbox as a pickup time. It was not uncommon for mail to fall behind schedule, in which case I would seek to make up time. On one such occasion I came around a corner at quite a clip and almost ran head-on into a car driven, once again, by John Q. Public. I'm sure that John Q. was very irritated with me about this near miss, but I'm also sure that he changed his mind afterwards if he woke up to the fact that he had been going the wrong way on a one-way street.

It was while driving around Ann Arbor to pick up mail that I ran into the biggest hailstones I've ever seen. They weren't record-breaking—only about the size of a ping pong ball—but big enough to keep me inside the truck for a while. During my sojourn in the truck, I had the privilege of listening to the almost unimaginable clatter of those hailstones striking the truck's steel roof.

Some nights, after completing my mail pickup route, I was unlucky enough to be the last driver to bring a truck back to the post office garage. Parking the last truck in the garage could sometimes be a time-consuming operation because there was just barely enough room in the garage for all of the trucks if each truck was snuggled up right close to its neighbors. Sometimes, in order to get the last truck in, it was necessary to jockey a few of the others around in order to get sufficient snuggling.

My post office truck driving also included, once in a while, delivering incoming mail to those greenish mailboxes you can still see around town (or at least around some towns). I want to describe the function of those greenish-colored mailboxes, and in order to do so, I need to talk some about "throwing" mail. If you aren't already into greenish mailboxes and throwing mail, the following discussion may satisfy the curiosity, if any, that you feel concerning such things.

Both incoming and outgoing mail was thrown in those days. During one Christmas vacation, my job at the post office was throwing outgoing mail. This consisted of standing in front of a large assemblage of pigeonholes, labeled with the names of various states and cities, and depositing one pile after another of outgoing mail into the appropriate pigeonholes. In the case of incoming mail, one throwing function I was aware of but did not perform myself was the sorting of piles of mail by depositing the mail into pigeonholes labeled with the numbers of the various mail routes in the town. This obviously required that the individual sorting the incoming mail be aware of the streets and addresses included in each route.

The final throwing function related to incoming mail and was something I became very familiar with. Each morning the incoming mail that had been allocated to a particular mail route was turned over to the mailman handling that route. (In those days, "mailman" was still an applicable term because, at least at the post offices where I worked, there were no female letter carriers.) The mailman would then sort the mail by address, making use of a multilevel rack labeled with all of the addresses on that particular mail route, each address being separated from the next one by a little metal divider. When the mailman finished throwing all of the mail to be delivered on his route that day, he would bundle it up and put it into various sacks that were to be taken by truck to be deposited in various greenish-colored mailboxes located along his route. All of the mail to be delivered on that day was handled as I just described, except for the mail to be delivered on the initial segment of the mail route, which, of course, was put into the letter carrier's mail sack when he headed out, on foot or by bus, to the starting point of his mail route.

If you'll continue to bear with me, I'll try to describe the function of the greenish mailboxes (for anyone who hasn't already figured it out). Briefly, these mailboxes were the places where the various mail carriers got refills for their mail sacks. The mail routes and the locations of the greenish mailboxes were planned and laid out in such manner that the mailman would arrive at such a mailbox each time he finished delivering a sack full of mail and would refill his sack from the mail placed in that box by the truck driver for the next segment of the mail route. In many cases a particular letter carrier would arrive at a particular greenish mailbox several times during his route, coming from a different direction each time.

Also, any greenish-colored mailbox located at the edge of a particular mail route was likely to serve one or more adjacent routes as well. Each sack of incoming mail placed in the box was, of course, labeled to indicate the mail route to which it belonged.

In connection with the planning of mail routes, I remember, as a little boy, seeing my dad from time to time poring over a street map of the city and marking it with pencils of various colors. Although I didn't realize it at the time, he was working on the layout of various mail routes.

As I said, I drove a truck and threw mail during my tours of duty at the two post offices, but my principal assignment was to deliver the mail. In that capacity, I walked a large percentage of the sidewalks of the two cities where I was a postal worker. The reason I covered so much different ground was, of course, that I didn't get assigned to a single route for an entire summer but instead pinch-hit for a number of vacationing mailmen on a number of different routes. This entailed my learning one mail route after another—for example, learning the location of mailboxes and mail slots that were not immediately apparent and learning the location of problem dogs. (More about dogs in a moment.) It sometimes seemed that just when I had learned a route, the regular letter carrier would return from vacation and I would move on to another route and start learning it.

Delivering mail provides one with lots of fresh air and sunshine but also provides certain disadvantages:

1. Weather: In rainy weather, I found it to be impossible to walk along carrying an umbrella and, at the same time, sorting through mail to segregate that to be delivered to a particular address. Accordingly, in the case of a real downpour, the mail might not go through until the mailman had stood on a porch or in another sheltered place waiting for the torrent to subside. When delivering mail at Christmastime, I found cold hands to be a bigger problem than snow, inasmuch as I didn't have skintight gloves and wasn't able to sort mail while walking down the street wearing the gloves I did have.
2. Magazines and samples: The day when *Life* magazine came out was particularly unpopular with mailmen because it was a big heavy magazine and there were lots of subscribers in those days.

Samples, often little boxes containing a tube of toothpaste or shampoo, were not heavy but were a problem by reason of being unwieldy. Thank goodness we didn't have to deal with the flood of catalogs that courses through the mails nowadays.

3. Dogs: An obvious problem. I've been a dog bite victim on a number of occasions, but, strangely enough, most of these incidents occurred when I was not carrying mail or otherwise employed by the post office. There were many more occasions, however, when I was carrying the mail and had cause for concern about the possibility of a dog bite, which, luckily, did not come to pass. I'll regale you with just a few dog stories.

My first experience of the dog-mailman conflict was on the dog's side, so to speak. When I was a kid, a dog belonging to the family of a friend of mine bit our mailman on two separate occasions. Evidently there was a local ordinance entitling every dog to one bite but providing that the dog could be put down if it bit more than once. The mailman insisted that the ordinance be applied in this case, and I remember how heartbroken my friend was at losing his dog.

Years later I became more empathetic with the mailman's viewpoint. On one mail route in my hometown that I carried for a time one summer, there was a dog that was tied to a garage by a chain about half as long as the driveway itself. Each day when I passed this place, the dog would go to the garage and then turn and run full tilt down the driveway toward me, growling and snarling all the way. Of course, each time he was caught short, and his head snapped back when he reached the end of the chain. Although this must have caused the dog some pain, it didn't stop him from repeating the procedure the next time I came by. I just thanked my lucky stars that the chain didn't break while I was carrying that route.

In another part of town, I walked up some porch steps one day to put some mail in the box and, as I reached the porch, became aware that a big German shepherd was coming at me. My first thought was, "Thank God he's tied up," but my second thought was, "Good God, he's *not* tied up." Luckily, the lady of the house came out onto the porch at the very moment when, it seemed to me, the dog was in midair on his final lunge toward me. She said, "Duke—down," or something to that effect, and the dog backed off.

On another day, as I started up a front sidewalk toward a house located on a mail route I was carrying for the first time, I saw a Doberman pinscher lying beside the walk, looking at me, and obviously feeling no fear. Saying to myself that the mail must go through, I kept walking, passed the dog (which just continued to lie there, looking at me), and delivered the mail. When I turned and walked back down the front sidewalk, I again passed the dog and noticed that he got up and started to follow me. Controlling my urge to run, I continued walking and delivering mail. The dog walked along right behind me, but I don't remember whether he accompanied me up to each house or waited out by the street while I made each mail delivery. In any event, he tagged along after me for about two blocks and then turned around and headed back. Somewhere along the line, a woman who lived in the neighborhood told me that every day the dog waited for the regular mailman to arrive at his (the dog's) house and then walked along with the mailman for a couple of blocks before returning home.

Three years later, when I spent the summer walking numerous mail routes in Ann Arbor, a very friendly little dog walked along with me for a while, and I even went so far as to pet him. At some point, he ran on ahead of me and went up on the porch of what I figured must be the house where his owners lived. When I arrived there and went up on the porch to deliver the mail, I leaned down to pet him again. He snarled, leaped toward my face, and might have got some nose if I hadn't quickly pulled myself up out of his reach. This seems to have been an example of a dog (like other entities, such as sports teams) being more self-confident and aggressive on home turf.

There's one more canine event I want to describe, even though it occurred long after my post office days. Once upon a time when I was jogging along a country road in suburbia, I passed a house that was set back about a hundred yards from the road and noticed a large dog and a couple of children standing by the house. When the dog saw me jogging by, he took off after me and caught up to me in moments. (That tells you something about the pace at which I jogged.) I continued at that pace and meanwhile issued to the dog a number of directives, which I had customarily used in my mailman days when under siege by one or more growling dogs, such as "Go away," "Scram," "Vamoose," and "Get lost." And perhaps I added a reference to Susie Q's brother, Fuh. Nothing worked; the dog continued growling and running along with me and bumping my legs. Finally, I said to the dog, "Bite my ass." And, wouldn't you know it—I had at last found a command the dog would and did obey.

Chapter 7

Mother(s)—In Fact and In-Law

My mother, unlike my father, lived to a ripe old age. She moved to California a couple of years after my father's death, and during the last decades of her life, my face-to-face contacts with her were accordingly infrequent and brief. For the same reason, my children knew her hardly at all. My family was an example of a rather common situation, where one set of grandparents is in close geographical proximity to the grandchildren and the other set of grandparents is not; the latter grandparents are thus virtual strangers to the grandchildren.

At the end of one of the few visits my mother made to us, my three daughters and I took her to the railroad station in Chicago to put her on the Santa Fe train back to Los Angeles. At this station there was an upstairs waiting room with floor-to-ceiling windows overlooking the train shed. I remember my three little girls in their matching dresses, standing at one of the windows, watching the train pull out, and waving good-bye as the tears streamed down their faces.

Like my father, my mother did not finish high school. But she became a very capable housewife, which is probably what most American women of her generation became. As the oldest girl in her family and the second oldest child of eight children, she became well prepared in her youth to handle that role. In addition to washing, ironing, cooking, cleaning, etc., some housewives in those days often went to bridge parties, and this was true in my mother's case. I have the impression that bridge parties are fewer and farther between nowadays, and no doubt one reason for this is that full-time housewives are likewise fewer and farther between.

In order to make time for bridge parties, Mom worked very hard and kept her household in good shape and her family well fed. We were particularly well fed on those occasions once or twice a year, when we had fried oysters and shoestring potatoes, delicacies that everyone looked forward to. However, I must have considered all of my mother's cooking lip-smacking good, for I couldn't begin to count how many times, during dinners, my dad told me to stop smacking.

Although I have no memory of the circumstances, it has been related to me that at some time in my early childhood, I woke up during the night and complained to my parents, who were also in bed at the time, that I couldn't sleep because the growling bear was disturbing me. My parents soon figured out that what was bothering me was my mother's snoring, and they consoled me as best they could.

In addition to being in charge of the snoring in the family, Mom was also in charge of medical matters. I've been told that when I was two or three years old, I was afflicted with a life-threatening case of scarlet fever, that Mom took care of me (with a doctor's help) until I weathered the storm, and that the rest of the family moved out of the house in the meantime. Mom also dispensed remedies for various other ailments—for example, substituting goat's milk for cow's milk in an effort to allay my eczema and painting my throat with iodine or forcing milk of magnesia down my throat for one reason or another. She also dispensed medical advice, one of my favorites being, "If you sit there too long, your insides will come out."

During one summer, Georgia and I had a problem with boils, and Mom came up with some foul-tasting pills that supposedly would remedy the problem. These pills tasted so bad that she let us take them with strawberry jam. The result was that Georgia and I steered clear of strawberry jam for some time thereafter. However, my mother's least successful remedy, hands down, has to be her application of Sloan's liniment to my sunburn on one occasion. Ouch!

Another time during my boyhood, Mom took me to an ear, nose, and throat specialist for treatment of some problem I had in that area. By the time I got out of that doctor's office, I thought I had been treated by some sort of infernal magician. The doctor put some type of apparatus into my mouth and/or nose and then instructed me to say "kay." When I did so,

I heard and felt what seemed like an explosion inside my head. He also instructed me to say "kick," which led to a double explosion. I don't recall how many repetitions there were of these damnable instructions, but when we finished the procedure, my concern was not just to check whether my head was on straight but to check whether my head was on at all. At that time, of course, I was not cognizant of epiglottises, uvulas, and Eustachian tubes or of the effect (or impact!) of the pronunciation of certain words upon one's oral and nasal structures and passageways.

My mother was far from the most liberal person in the world and was rather unhappy with me one day when she learned that, on the way home from grade school, I had engaged in a short wrestling match with a black kid by the name of Norman and ended up in the gutter with him on top of me. He was my classmate and was the first African American to attend our school.

As it turned out, Norman was quite a good athlete, perhaps the best in the school for his age. My reaction to this was not, "Colored guys are really good athletes," but, rather, "Norman is a really good athlete."

He and I were friendly during the time he was at the school, but he lived a half-mile or so east of my neighborhood, and we didn't hang around together outside of school hours. When we had our brief wrestling match, we were just horsing around and no quarrel or anger was involved. As a matter of fact, I felt honored that Norman would bother to wrestle with a nonathlete like me.

Since most of my parental contact during the day was with my mother rather than my father, she had occasion, from time to time, to dispense discipline, most of it verbal. When it came to physical punishment, she generally followed the "You just wait until your father gets home" approach. You may recall, however, that there was at least one time when she washed my mouth out with soap.

Rod told me of another episode where it seems likely that Mom meted out physical punishment, although I have no personal memory of what happened. It seems that Rod was on the way to join his buddies somewhere when Mom told him he would need to stay home for a while tending to two-year-old Paul, who was out in the yard. Rod evidently had a saw (why, I don't know) and at some point held it near his baby brother's throat while he had some such train of thought as, "I'd like to saw your head off, you little squirt, for keeping me from going off to play with my pals." Just at this moment, our mother glanced out the window, saw the scene I have just described, and went ballistic. Rod suffered the consequences.

Mom went ballistic in another way when she was told of the death of her mother, and this was probably the most traumatic and sad scene I've ever witnessed. At the time of her death, my grandmother had been living several blocks away from us at the home of Mom's younger sister Dorothy and her family. Grandma died in her sleep on the night before her birthday, when a party was to take place at Dorothy's house. In the morning, while we were getting ready to go to the birthday party, Dorothy arrived at our house and said to my mother, "Mama's gone away." At this, my mother collapsed and began writhing around on the floor, all the while screaming, "No, no, no." I felt so sorry for her…and so helpless.

My mother spent the last year or so of her own life at a very nice retirement home in Orange County, California. She was by no means bedridden, but she was quite old, and her faculties were not as sharp as in former days. She also had memory problems. For example, for several years prior to her death, she had a practice of hiding her purse somewhere in her home, forgetting where she had put it, and then searching for it.

During the short time she lived in the retirement home, she was befriended by a widower by the name of Jimmy, who was also a resident at the home and several years younger than Mom. In her letters and in the telephone conversations I had with her periodically, she mentioned Jimmy often, but she assured me that she and Jimmy did not plan to marry. I finally met Jimmy when Nancy and I visited my mother about six weeks before her death. (The timing of our visit was coincidental, for we had no inkling that her death was that imminent.) At any rate, Nancy and I agreed that Jimmy was one of the sweetest guys we had ever met. We were not so tactless as to question him about his relationship with my mother, but it became apparent during our visit that Jimmy was just a very nice man who enjoyed the time he spent with her and knew that she enjoyed it as well, that he had no intention of marrying her or anyone else, and that the possibility of marrying her had undoubtedly never crossed his mind (although the thought of such a possibility had evidently become implanted in hers).

Many years earlier I had been called upon to tell Mom of the death of Georgia's firstborn, a beautiful baby girl named Shelley, who was afflicted with spina bifida and died when she was about ten months old. Mother lived in California, was close to Georgia geographically and otherwise, and just doted on this poor little baby. At the time of Shelley's death, which was probably ten days or so before my daughter Pat was born, Mom had just arrived to visit and help out for a week or two after our baby's arrival. One evening I received a call from California telling me of Shelley's death, and it was, of course, obvious that I should tell Mom of the tragedy instead of letting her hear about it over the phone. So, after hanging up the phone, I put my arms around my mother, held her tight to prevent her from collapsing to the floor, and told her the terrible news. Naturally, she headed right back to California.

A few years earlier, when Georgia was about to get married in southern California, my mother-in-law, Lucille (and her very elderly father) did something very nice for me. Because my dad was no longer living, Georgia wanted Rod to give her away at her wedding. Rod lived in North Carolina with Fran (his first wife) and their two young daughters and could not afford the airfare to California. Georgia turned next to me, a law student at Michigan being supported by my wife and by my own meager earnings from my summertime job at the Ann Arbor post office. So I also had to decline, for financial reasons, the chance to give away my baby sister. When Lucille learned of the situation, she arranged for her father to give me the two or three hundred dollars it cost to fly from Detroit to Los Angeles in those days, and I was able to walk Georgia down the aisle after all.

From time to time I wore pants without putting on a belt, and on one occasion Lucille noticed I was beltless. She turned to Barbara, who was also present, and inquired as to whether I wore belts. I thought it strange that she asked Barbara, for I felt well qualified to answer the question. I could have explained that I went beltless from time to time in order to meet the requirements imposed on candidates for the No-Belt Prize.

Many years later I ran into a similar situation when Barbara, our daughter Pat, and I were in downtown Boston near Faneuil Hall and found ourselves standing very near to Ted Kennedy. We noticed that he was wearing neither a belt nor suspenders, but we made no inquiries regarding the matter.

After my first marriage ended and I married Nancy, her mother, Lorraine, became my mother-in-law. Lorraine lived alone and thus had no one to talk to most of the time. So when she came to our place for a visit, she talked to Nancy *a lot*. During the course of their conversations, I from time to time made an observation, and Lorraine from time to time told me that I was interrupting her. My response usually was to the effect that if I didn't interrupt her, it would be impossible for me to speak at any time during her visit. I'm kidding about this, of course, and she loved it when I kidded her. But not very much.

Lorraine came up with a quip of her own now and then, sometimes inadvertently. I'll cite just one example, which happened when Lorraine and Nancy and I stopped to pick up a close friend of Nancy's who was going on some sort of excursion with us. This lady was from down south and was rather heavy set. As she climbed into the car and was asked how she was doing, she responded that she was "feelin' fat and sassy." Lorraine returned the following zinger: "You're not sassy."

Chapter 8

The Little Fisherman and the Acrophobe

The reference to "little fisherman" in the title of this chapter refers not to the magnitude of me but to my minuscule achievements in the art and/or science of angling. As in the case of golf, I was an incompetent dilettante when it came to fishing. As a matter of fact, it could be said that, if you think I'm a lousy golfer, you should see me fish.

Over the years there were a number of vacation trips that involved or were supposed to involve fishing. One year our vacation headquarters were a cabin on a lake in the interior of the Cape Cod peninsula. A couple of times some of the children and I went out in a small boat to fish in this lake, with very little success. My memory is that virtually the only fish we caught were eels. In any instance where such a catch was made by one of the children, I remember how her or his excitement at feeling something tugging on the line was transformed into horror when the line came up out of the water and disclosed this writhing snakelike thing. The first time this occurred I decided that I like eels about as much as I like snakes, but I was nevertheless designated by the unanimous vote of the children to be the person to remove the hook from the eel and put it (the eel) back in the lake.

We didn't do any ocean fishing while at Cape Cod, but a few years later Barbara and I went out in what's called a party boat off the Maryland coast while spending part of a vacation at Ocean City. This was not really deep-sea fishing and involved a large number of people fishing from one boat in close proximity to one another. I recall that somebody apparently hooked a skate, which accordingly went berserk, with the result being ten or twenty fishing lines becoming one tangled mess.

I have no recollection of catching any fish during this Maryland outing, for I became involved in something entirely different than fishing. At some point I noticed a boy lying on a bench on deck and holding a plastic bag near his face. At first I just noticed this without thinking about it. Shortly thereafter, I realized that this boy was no doubt seasick. My next step was to think that he had become seasick because of the way the boat was rocking back and forth. My next step was to think that I could understand how that rocking motion could make one seasick. My next step…well, you get the idea.

Something similar happened in a later year during a vacation trip with our two boys. While we were staying at a cabin in the Black Hills, we went fishing one day at a small pond that was kept stocked with plenty of fish. I don't remember the extent to which I succeeded in catching fish, but I do recall the fish-cleaning station provided by the pond owner. This station was manned by a young man whose mandate was to spend all day cleaning the fish caught by the customers—and he was fast, man! While he cleaned whatever fish our group had caught, we watched his knife moving back and forth, and in and out, and watched the resulting blood and guts spewing and spilling. Pretty soon we noticed that our younger son, Tom, was turning rather green, but we managed to get him away from there before any chuck came up.

Two other so-called fishing trips provide ample confirmation that my status as a little fisherman is well deserved. Be that as it may, one of the trips, with our sons, was to Bull Shoals Lake, Arkansas, which I (fool that I was) regarded as a place where absolutely anybody could catch plenty of fish. The trip to Arkansas involved travel on U.S. Highway No. 60, and in this connection I need to digress a bit.

My former wife was an acrophobe, and some of her more disturbing instances of being frightened while situated on high or precipitous places had occurred on Route 60. I believe the first such episode occurred when we drove through the Salt River canyon in Arizona. A couple of years later we drove across West Virginia on Route 60. I don't believe this involved any cliffside driving, but it did involve going uphill and down, over and over again, which was bothersome to her. Finally, on another trip, we drove on Route 60 through the Kentucky River canyon. This isn't much of a canyon by Rocky Mountain standards, but it is enough of a canyon by acrophobic standards.

Please understand that I did not plan our routes of travel with the objective of driving (yes, driving) Barbara to distraction. However, by the time I started planning our route to Bull Shoals Lake, I had the "Route 60 connection" in mind. As far as I could tell from the map, that part of southern Missouri through which we would be traveling on Route 60 appeared to be relatively flat, and we decided to chance that highway again.

When we reached Route 60 on our way to Arkansas, it proved to be no problem from an acrophobic standpoint. The road was indeed relatively flat, free of precipices, and altogether a fine highway. However, when we arrived at the bridge where Route 60 crosses the St. Francis River in southeast Missouri, something happened which demonstrated that flat Route 60 could sometimes be much more of a problem than precipitous Route 60. We were involved in an auto accident.

This was a very strange auto accident indeed, for we were rear-ended by a vehicle that must have been a quarter of a mile or more behind us when we came to a stop in traffic. Here's how it happened: As we approached the bridge, we saw that a wide farm implement was very slowly coming across the bridge in the other direction and partially blocking our lane. Two or three cars ahead of us were stopped and waiting for the farm implement to clear the bridge, and we came to a stop behind these cars. While we were waiting in this line of cars, I noticed in the rearview mirror that a vehicle still some distance behind us was approaching at a rather high speed. My thought process during the next few moments went something like this: "I assume that vehicle will stop. I hope it will stop. I pray it will stop. My God, it's *not* going to stop!" In the course of these thoughts, I made appropriate communications to Barbara and our two sons, who were in the back seat of our Buick station wagon, so we were as ready as possible when the impact came.

Our car was hit on the left rear corner by a vehicle that was some kind of a little pickup truck, I think. The driver, an elderly man who obviously was not big in the depth perception, judgment, and reaction-time departments, did at least veer at the last second, so that only the left rear of our car was smashed. No one seemed to have been hurt, though there was glass all over the place, and our car was drivable and the gas tank intact.

There were, of course, a few things to attend to at the accident scene, and these included a decision by us as to whether we would continue on to Arkansas or turn around and head home. We decided to continue on, and it soon became important that we continue on rapidly, inasmuch as we were now traveling in a partly open-air station wagon with a tail full of all sorts of things that should preferably be kept dry and inasmuch as (naturally) the sky was clouding up and looking quite threatening. We did make it to a hardware store in the next town before the rain started, and we got the new openings in the car covered by clear plastic in time. During the remainder of this vacation trip, we learned that traveling in a fully loaded station wagon is not nearly as pleasurable when the tailgate doesn't operate. In particular, it is not at all convenient to load or unload the car under those circumstances.

It's easy to tell, from the length of the preceding digression, that I'm not eager to talk further about my fishing nonexploits. But because I indicated at the outset that a subject of this chapter is fishing, I'd better get back to that subject. We did spend a week at a resort on the north shore of Bull Shoals Lake and, I believe, went fishing virtually every day. My catch for the week was one small fish, and that poor devil didn't take my bait but unfortunately snagged his gill on my hook while swimming along minding his own business. It seems clear that the locations where we fished were wrong from either a horizontal or vertical standpoint, or perhaps both, for Barbara and the boys didn't fare much better than I in the fish-catching department.

You would think that the Bull Shoals Lake experience would have cured me, but it didn't. A few years later Barbara and I took a trip with friends named Carl and Elinor to a lake in the Ontario wilderness north of Sault Ste. Marie and east of Wawa. Luckily for our friends, they usually went out in one boat (the fish-catching boat) and Barbara and I went out in another (the non-fish-catching boat).

Each morning the people who operated the fishing camp would advise the current visitors as to where the fish were expected to be biting that day and where the shore lunch would be served. Also, although the camp operators did not bring in a noted outdoorsman—like Al Fresco, for instance—to educate the would-be anglers, they did provide some instructions concerning recommended fish-catching methods.

All to no avail, in my case. Though I believe I situated our boat in the suggested areas and used the recommended methods, the results were as usual—our catch was somewhere between few fish and none. The fish (caught by other people) that we ate at the shore lunches were delicious, and these lunches were delightful once I got past the initial embarrassment of trying to sneak our minuscule contribution of fish into the fish-frying area without too many others seeing just how puny our contribution was.

Besides the food, there were other good things about this Ontario trip. The country was beautiful, and the loons (I speak of the feathered variety) were plentiful. I had previously seen and heard loons in northern Wisconsin, where they seemed to be few and far between and never nearby, and I had always loved to hear their call. In Ontario there were scads of loons, and they were often close by. Sometimes there were two or three of them in the water right near our boat.

In addition, though I had no success in fishing at the Ontario lake, I did learn several rules relating to fishing: (1) When you are fishing out of one side of the boat and your wife is fishing out of the other side, try to avoid getting your lines tangled together under the boat. (2) Connect your fishing line to the leader by a properly tied, secure knot, so that if a fish takes your bait, he cannot pull bait, hook, and leader free of your line unless he is strong enough to break it. (3) If you do catch a few fish and keep them in a creel in the water while you continue to fish, remember to put the creel into a bucket of water in the boat before starting the motor and moving the boat—especially if the line on the creel is so long that it is possible for the creel and line to foul the propeller.

Although most of the time our friends fished together in one boat and the Gablers in another, there were a few occasions when Carl and I fished together. I particularly remember one evening—I believe our last evening at the lake—when we went to fish at the edge of a fairly large area full of reeds and lily pads, because we had been told that the big ones were really biting in that area. The big ones were indeed biting, but we didn't stay very long, because the big ones we encountered were mosquitoes rather than fish!

On the way back to the lodge, Carl ran the motor and I leaned back in the bow of the boat and watched the western sky and tried to whistle "Canadian Sunset" as twilight approached. The whistling was pretty bad, but the sky was pretty pretty.

Chapter 9

Timberlane

For a number of years, my former wife's parents, Money and Lucille, operated a resort in far northern Wisconsin known as Timberlane. It consisted of a number of cabins scattered through the wooded grounds and a lodge right next to South Turtle Lake, with kitchen, dining room, living room, office, and bar on the first floor; recreation room in the basement; and numerous bedrooms upstairs.

During these years, Timberlane was a frequent vacation destination for my family. While we were there, Barbara and I spent most of our time looking after and finding ways to entertain the children, but we also gave some help to Money and Lucille at the lodge. As the children got older, they pitched in as well. My more extended family became involved in Timberlane one summer, when Rod's younger daughter, Paula, was sixteen. She and a friend came all the way from California to work as waitresses at the lodge.

The next year, my two older daughters went up to Timberlane by themselves to help Grandma and Grandpa (and to have fun, too). Laura was twelve and Pat ten. They traveled by bus and had to change buses at Madison. This was the first time they had gone any distance without Mommy or Daddy, and it was an emotional—and proud—moment for me when they waved good-bye as the bus pulled away.

A special feature at Timberlane was the various excursions planned by Lucille and Money for guests, both adult and children. One frequent excursion was a nighttime drive to a dump located in the woods a few miles away. Some excursion, you say? Well, it really was, for nighttime was the time when the bears congregated at the dump.

Another little trip we took brought us to a place called Lake in the Clouds, located about sixty miles north of Timberlane in the hills bordering Lake Superior in the Upper Peninsula of Michigan. The thing to do at Lake in the Clouds was to walk up a hill until you found yourself on the top of a cliff overlooking the little lake hundreds of feet below. From this point you could also see, through a gap in the hills, a bit of Lake Superior a couple of miles away. A pleasant aftermath was an early evening picnic on the beach at Lake Superior, featuring views of the sun setting beyond the lake and of a beaver or other aquatic mammal swimming by.

Timberlane was somewhat more than 400 miles from where we lived in northern Illinois, and in those days most of this distance was traveled on two-lane roads. This meant that much of the travel time was spent in one long string of cars after another, with one or more cars at the front traveling more slowly than the following drivers desired and with the latter eagerly awaiting opportunities to pass. Well, at least there were fewer trucks on the roads then.

With Timberlane being a resort on a lake, it was, unfortunately, virtually incumbent upon me to do some fishing. However, all that I will add here concerning that subject is a mention of a birthday present my in-laws gave me one summer. Money hired a guide, and the three of us went out muskie fishing. This type of fishing involved lures that were bigger than almost any fish I've ever caught. It would probably go without saying that no fish were caught on this expedition. But at least I didn't catch Money either. As you may recall, I had previously hit him with one of my shots while golfing, so it was with some relief that I managed to avoid snagging him with any of my casts while fishing.

During one summer, Barbara and the kids stayed at Timberlane for several weeks, and I commuted back and forth on weekends. One night, when I was heading home by myself, there was a heavy fog for about 200 miles. Luckily for me, almost no one else was on the road—as far as I could tell.

There were two years when I went up to Timberlane in early October to help Money and Matt, a neighbor of his, close up the resort for the winter. The drill on these occasions was early to bed, early to rise, work your tail off all morning, and then in the afternoon go over to the tavern in the nearby village to drink beer, eat peanuts and popcorn, and watch the World Series. (It was still played in the afternoon in those days.) One of the World Series we watched under these circumstances is a rather famous series, between the Pirates and the Yankees, won by the Pirates on Bill Mazeroski's home run in the last half of the ninth inning of the seventh game.

In one of the two years when I went up to Timberlane in October, I had to leave before all the winterizing work was done, because of business commitments. So I took the cheese train from far northern Wisconsin to Chicago, instead of waiting until later to come back in the car with Money and Matt. This was a thirteen-hour train ride, though a lot of it could more properly be denoted a "train sit." For example, the train was stationary in the Green Bay railroad yard for close to two hours.

The only other time I've been in or near Green Bay also involved transportation, when I changed planes at the Green Bay airport in the course of a business trip a number of years later. While I was seated during the layover, I had occasion to view the following declaration (with which I agree), inscribed on the inside of the door I was facing: "I'd rather have one bottle in front of me than one frontal lobotomy."

Chapter 10

Three Sisters

My three oldest children are my daughters: Laura, Pat, and Gail. Pat's official name is Patricia, but she was called Pat or Patty almost all the time. In addition, her father called her Patsy, Patsareno, or Patsarama from time to time.

Through their childhood years, the girls did things together, did things separately, fought, squabbled, formed and ended alliances and ententes, got along with one another, and failed to get along with one another. However, if and when the need arose, and regardless of the then current status of their relationships with one another, it seemed that they could find a way to unite against someone who at the moment was the common enemy; no doubt you can figure out who that often was. Something else that all three girls shared was their delight in welcoming a little brother to the family.

Before I launch into a description of other incidents involving my daughters, I'll favor you with a few observations regarding parent-child relationships, based on my experience:

1. During the years when my children were growing up, a standard piece of expert advice was that parents should find the time and make themselves available to hear about and discuss their children's problems. I believe I did this and also made my availability known to my children, but what I found for the most part is that the children did not themselves have the time, or did not have the desire, to talk things over with me. And this finding was consistent

with my memory of how things were when I was on the child side of the equation.

2. When our children were young, Barbara and I worked hard to make sure that our kids were well-behaved when outside of our household, and we succeeded. For example, we received frequent compliments from strangers as to the good behavior of the five children while seated with us at a table in a restaurant. Much of the credit for the result should go to the children's willingness to listen and obey and to the impact on the younger children's conduct of the example and admonitions of the older ones. I have no idea whether a well-behaved young child is more likely to grow up to be a better adult human being. And I don't care, for good behavior on the part of young children is an end in itself. If it is also conducive to the child becoming a better adult, that, of course, is a plus.
3. In a family including more than one child, it seems to me that an unusually large percentage of the parents' (or at least the father's) memories of the babyhood and tothood of the children will relate to the babyhood and tothood of the firstborn child. Perhaps the memorable incidents of the first child's early days become firmly lodged in the memory before the births of additional children lead to an ever-increasing jumble of incidents and memories that become more and more mixed up in one's memory (or forgettory?). I have been speaking of the difficulty I have of ascribing to a particular later-born child a particular cute saying or action or a particular event, and this obviously doesn't apply to an incident that, by its very nature, necessarily relates to a particular child. An example of the latter occurred when Ed was delivered by a doctor who was aware that we already had three daughters. When the doctor displayed Ed to me in the fathers' waiting room, he exclaimed, "Look, he's got a handle!"

In any event, I remember quite a few cute and/or funny sayings and doings by Laura during her tothood, and not so many in the case of the other kids. When Laura was learning to talk, she naturally didn't completely understand the meaning of many of the words she used, and this led to some interesting word usages on her part. On occasions when she and her mother and I would take walks when she was very young, sometimes I would notice that she seemed to be getting tired and would ask her a question that sounded like, "Want Daddy to carry ya?" After this had happened a few times, she began to take the initiative and, when she wanted to be carried, would turn and raise her arms toward me and say, "Daddy carry ya." Laura also made what I think was a cute misuse of the word "much," as the equivalent of "amount." For example, when asked how much ice cream she wanted, she might say that she wanted the "same much" as her mommy was having.

When she was two or three years old, Laura would sometimes join her parents in bed in the early morning, and her parents wouldn't always wake up right away. I remember one morning when I finally awakened, and Laura laughed and said, "Daddy, you got a big finger on your bottom and I tickled it." Moving right along... On another occasion I apparently touched Laura on the back with more vigor than she had anticipated, and she objected to my hitting her. I told her that I had not hit her and that it was a love pat. Laura's response was, "I don't love it."

One time, after the arrival of Patty, we had a meal that included potato pancakes (which were also called, at least at that time, potato patties). When Laura inquired as to what the new-to-her type of food on her plate was, I told her it was potato patties. Her response was, "No, it's potato Laura's."

Even long after Laura learned to talk, she had trouble with certain sounds or words. The most memorable instance of this was her inability, when she was a tot, to pronounce the word "coffee." She instead said "cawpee." I worked with her on this over and over again, telling her that she should say, "ff...ff...coffee." Her response (until she finally overcame the problem) was to say, "ff...ff...cawpee."

Laura had difficulty with another word shortly after we moved into our first house when she was about four years old. She came into the house one day and announced that a neighborhood boy had called her and Patty "little ships". Little did she know that her own father had at one time regarded himself as a coinventor of the word the neighborhood boy had actually used.

About a year before the happening I just described, Laura had a problem with a couple of little boys in another neighborhood, while the older girls and I were staying at my brother's home for a few days at the time Gail was born. Being away from home, Laura did not have a lot to do, and I encouraged her to go outdoors and play with other children who lived in the area. Laura did so, but when she approached the two boys, one of them tried to run into her with his tricycle and both appeared to be saying unfriendly things to her. I remember watching her out the window as she put her hands on the front wheel of the trike in an effort to keep this boy from bumping her. I felt so sorry for her and wanted so much to go out there and take those boys and knock their heads together, but I believed that I should not intervene. A father feels very sad when he thinks he could help his child but feels that he mustn't.

The youngest girl, Gail, had difficulty pronouncing the letter "s" at the beginning of words up to the time when she was five or six years old. She would accordingly come up with such statements as, "I'm going to 'ing a 'ong at 'unday 'cool." Barbara was finally able to help Gail overcome this problem with the aid of a mirror. She would sit beside Gail on the davenport with the mirror on their laps. Barbara would then show Gail how the lips are formed in order to make the "s" sound. Gail could see in the mirror how her mother's lips were formed and could then try to put her lips in the same form and pronounce the "s" sound. Ultimately it worked.

Gail was more or less in charge of a species of entertainment the children (or at least the girls) provided for their parents once in a while. These presentations were called "Gail Gabler and Guests" and consisted of skits, songs, etc., which were put on in an area of the basement that was curtained off between acts, so to speak, by means of a bedspread hung over a clothesline. In putting on these entertainments, Gail and her older sisters made frequent and substantial use of the dress-up clothes and accessories contained in an old chest, which, I believe, had been provided by Barbara's mother.

Pat provided her parents with one of the thrills of a lifetime when she came out of the recovery room after some surgery she had when she was fifteen years old. This was not a life-threatening situation but was a very long operation, involving the transplant of bone from Pat's hip to both of her jaws. After waiting anxiously for hours during the surgery, her mother and I were virtually transported with joy to see her safely back in her hospital room afterwards, with her jaws wired shut and her head almost completely covered with bandages. Pat could greet us only with her eyes and a very faint murmur, but it was a greeting that produced a lot of emotion in me then and remains a very emotional moment in my memory now.

A few years later, Pat supplied a good example of quick-wittedness, relating to a medical procedure involving me this time. This occurred when she inquired as to the results of my first visit to a proctologist. I told her that nothing much had happened and that the doctor had just *analyzed* things. Pat then expressed the hope that everything would be *rectified*.

The first house we bought was in Elgin about a mile away from the railroad station where I caught a commuter train to take me to my job at a law firm in Chicago. For many years, almost every morning when I left the house to walk to the train station, one or several of the children would stand on a davenport at a downstairs window, wave good-bye to me as I walked away, and watch until I was out of sight. And, of course, I turned and waved back several times also. Laura was the instigator of this, to me, wonderful tradition and the most regular participant.

Laura was also the prime mover of something else I recall very fondly—being met by one or more of my daughters while walking home from the train station in the evening. Most often it was just Laura who would walk part of the way to the station to meet me, but Patty came with her on some occasions and Gail on less frequent occasions. These meetings, of course, were a sometime thing, for they occurred only when the weather was good and even then did not happen on anything like a daily basis. However, I got in the habit of looking way down the street ahead of me while walking home, in hopes of spotting one or more small figures blocks away heading toward me. Whenever I did see what I was looking for, my heart (if I may wax poetic while remaining very sincere) leapt. In later years, when Nancy and I lived in Chicago and I commuted via the Chicago elevated system, I got essentially the same feelings on those occasions when Nancy was waiting for me at the elevated station in the evening or met me while I was walking home from the station.

To return to the days of yore, occasionally when I went to the office on a Saturday, some of the children (most often the three girls) would accompany me. During the morning I would sit on one side of the desk doing lawyer work while the children would be lined up along the other side of the desk, reading, writing, drawing, coloring, etc. And behaving very well, I will add. We generally brought our lunches and ate them in my office, and in the afternoon we would do something that was a special treat—for example, visit a museum, ride the subway, take in a Cubs game, or go to a zoo. On one of these Saturdays, the three girls and Ed and I went to a ball game. The girls were very interested in the game, but Ed, who was probably three years old, was soon fast asleep. The sight of this little boy sound asleep amidst his three excited and noisy big sisters elicited many a smile from the people sitting near us.

I've been describing some of the roses that I have smelled along the way. And, after the passage of all these years, thinking about them—and, even more so, writing about them—brings back at least a whiff of their fragrance.

Chapter 11

Entertaining the Kids

This subject will be touched on here and elsewhere, though I'm sure I can't remember everything that Barbara and/or I did with the purpose of entertaining our children.

When it came time to read to my young daughters, two of their favorites were "Little Black Sambo" and one of the Oz books that involved a password that I don't remember exactly but was something like Keekie Kookaroo. One thing the girls especially liked about "Little Black Sambo" was my use of a big gruff voice when Mr. Tiger was talking and a little squeaky voice when Sambo was pleading with Mr. Tiger to spare him.

When the kids were young, we developed a game of our own that we called, for some unremembered reason, Wild Monkey. This involved some or all of the kids, whoever might be available at the time, running at and jumping on and wrestling with their daddy and the whole group of us rolling around on the floor. Obviously, as the kids grew, Daddy tended to become less interested in Wild Monkey.

A really good game for children of all ages, from three years old on up, was Blockhead. For the uninitiated, this entailed one of the players selecting as a base one of a set of little blocks of wood of various shapes, each player in turn placing another block on the structure rising from the base, and the player whose block caused the structure to tumble becoming the blockhead. We even got Rod involved in Blockhead during one of his visits, when he took on Ed and Ed's sisters while waiting for the time to come for me to take him to the airport.

Indoors, parents and kids played various other games involving boards or cards or both, including Candyland, Clue, Sleuth, and Spades. When the kids got into their teens, Spades got to be a very popular game in our household for several years. There were a few vacations we took with the boys when we played Spades each night for a couple of hours. We kept a cumulative score of the Spades games, though one of the vacations we split into a Wild West Spades Tournament and a Great Northern Spades Tournament. By this time, the girls were old enough to stay home alone and were involved in summer jobs and other activities. Besides, the girls by then had no doubt had their fill of battlefield tours. (More about battlefields shortly.)

On wintertime days when there was a lot of snow on the ground, the girls and Ed liked to play Fox and Geese. Usually Ed was the easiest goose for the fox to catch, and not just because he was the youngest player. For some reason he began to laugh whenever he was being chased. The longer the chase continued, the harder he laughed. Invariably he would end up falling down and then lying in the snow, laughing, while he was tagged and thus transformed into the fox. I don't remember Tom being involved in the Fox and Geese games. Perhaps he was too young or preferred not to risk duplicating his older brother's performance.

Another chasing game we liked to play was holly. Sometimes the kids and I played holly with a high school friend of mine, also named Ed, and his kids at the home that he and his wife owned out in the nearby countryside. Friend Ed and I particularly enjoyed the game during the years when we could outrun all the children.

The place owned by my friend Ed and his wife had a real big yard and so was also an ideal place for softball when our families got together or there was a larger gathering. At the first home that Barbara and I owned, we considered the yard to be big enough for at least in-family softball. However, at some point Laura demonstrated that our yard had ceased to be large enough, for she started hitting the ball beyond a group of evergreen trees at the back end of our lot. (It was at this point that she became a switch-hitter, trying—though often still failing—to keep the ball in our yard.) There was, of course, a period of time when I probably could have hit the ball even farther than Laura, but I generally pitched to the kids and didn't come to the plate at all.

When the kids were young, we took them to kiddie parks, which were sort of mini-amusement parks, with very tame rides and other activities for small children. Later we graduated, briefly, to the Riverview amusement park in Chicago, with roller coasters and other exciting things.

Gail was the first of the children to go to Riverview. When she was about eight years old, she had a problem with her ears that entailed a few visits to a specialist in Chicago. On the way home from one of these doctor appointments, Gail and I stopped at Riverview for a while. Not too long afterwards, the whole family visited Riverview. And not too long after that, Riverview closed forever.

Hiking was another activity for the kids, both during vacations and while we were homebound. One of the memorable vacation-time hikes I took with several of the children occurred at Cumberland Gap. We walked through the woods to the place where Kentucky, Tennessee, and Virginia meet. There we found a metal plaque embedded in concrete and showing the state boundaries meeting at a point, so we danced and pranced from state to state for a few minutes.

The sites of other long or short hikes (or walks) with one or more of the children during vacations over the years included the following:

- Civil War, Revolutionary War, and Indian wars battlefields, the most picturesque of which was located at the north end of Lookout Mountain, overlooking Chattanooga, Tennessee;
- gardens and/or mazes at Monticello (Thomas Jefferson's home), Mount Vernon (George Washington's home), and colonial Williamsburg, all in Virginia;
- several caves, including the historic tour of Mammoth Cave (Kentucky);
- a high sand dune at Saugatuck, Michigan, with the benefit of a staircase;
- beaches at Ocean City, Maryland; Cape Cod (Massachusetts); and Cape Hatteras (North Carolina);
- streets and the Mall in Washington, DC; the streets of the French Quarter in New Orleans; and the Freedom Trail in Boston;

- up and down hills at Mt. Wachusett (Massachusetts); at Devil's Lake (Wisconsin); and near a cabin we rented in the Black Hills of South Dakota;
- Mormon sites in Palmyra, New York; and Nauvoo, Illinois;
- Goat Island (New York), in the middle of the Niagara River;
- to and from a place known as the Chalk Mine in the woods of Virginia;
- portions of the Natchez Trace in Mississippi and the Oregon Trail at Scottsbluff, Nebraska; and
- part of the way across the little bitty Mississippi River, by stepping from rock to rock, where the river originates, flowing out of Lake Itasca in Minnesota.

The beach at Cape Cod was the site of a short hike that I took with just one of the children, Gail. We first saw the beach from a bluff that seemed to be 100 feet or more above it, and Gail expressed a desire to walk, slide, etc., down to the beach. The rest of us, no doubt thinking mainly of the return trip, did not share Gail's feeling, but I finally agreed to go with her. My memory is that we did indeed do more sliding than walking on the way down and that the return journey was not nearly as much fun.

While we were at the beach near Cape Hatteras, fourteen-year-old Pat took a snapshot of me while I (unaware of being photographed) was sitting on a big piece of driftwood and looking out at the sea. The next Christmas she surprised me with a gift of a very much blown-up and framed version of this snapshot. It remained a treasure of mine for many years, during which the photo became very much faded. In the meantime, Pat presented me with a smaller and much clearer version of the original photograph.

Around home, when Laura was three or four years old, I took much shorter hikes with her on a regular basis. On most Sundays she and I would walk to and from a neighborhood store about six blocks away in order to buy the newspaper. What made these excursions more fun than the usual daughter-father walk was that we played a modified form of hide-and-seek on the way home. All that this involved was both of us hiding behind a tree, peeking out at the other, and then running to other trees along the route home and repeating the process again and again. It doesn't sound like much, but it was enough to yield some joy to a little girl—and to a daddy.

When we were at home, some or all of the family took hikes from time to time at parks or along a trail called the Prairie Path, which was the spruced-up right-of-way of a defunct electric railroad. Probably our favorite hiking place was a local park that was full of trees and underbrush and had pretty much been left in a wild state. There were trails and a creek running through the park and also a number of places where trees had fallen down and lay across the creek. Part of the fun was to see to what extent it was possible for the children to cross the creek by walking and/or "skooching" along these fallen trees. At the north end of this park was a ridge, and generally the wind-up to our hikes was a clamber up to the top of this ridge, past trees, bushes, and underbrush, without benefit of a trail. When we reached the top of the ridge and looked at the scene below, what to our wondering eyes should appear but…a busy expressway!

Chapter 12

The Silent Dog

My customary means of commuting to my downtown workplace during the years Nancy and I lived in Chicago was the rapid transit system known as the el. For quite a few years my route to the el station took me down a brick alley that runs past the backyards of a group of row houses. Weather permitting, on most days during these years, a large white dog could be found lying next to the back gate of one of these row houses whenever I passed by. The dog resembled a Samoyed but seemed larger, and I surmised that the dog might be a mix including husky or malamute. In any event, the dog was large and white.

Sometimes when I walked by, the dog would look up at me, and sometimes she seemed to pay no attention to me, looking past me or elsewhere. In either case, the dog made no sound but either silently regarded me or silently disregarded me. I believe the only time I heard the dog make a sound was an occasion when I heard her bark, in what I considered to be a happy manner, while one of her owners was out in the backyard with her.

I soon got in the habit of saying something along the lines of, "Hey, Buddy," when I passed by the silent, prone dog, but whether she looked at me or not seemed to have no relationship to whether I spoke to the dog or not. (You've probably noticed that I have referred to the dog as a female, but this is information that I did not have until years after I began walking along the alley and saying, "Hey, Buddy.")

I noticed that some other people stopped to pet the dog and that she sometimes stood up, as if to demonstrate her receptiveness to being petted by a particular person. For years I confined myself to "Hey, Buddy" and didn't pet the dog. I had the attitude that it was not my business to pet somebody else's dog. I had been a dog owner in the past but not for many years, and at some point it occurred to me that this silent white dog had become my favorite dog in the world. There were plenty of other dogs in the neighborhood where Nancy and I lived, including a Saint Bernard, a couple pugs, a golden retriever, and a mutt or two who dwelt at other row houses along the same alley. However, none of them were in the habit (or allowed by their owners to be in the habit) of lying by their back gates on most days and thus becoming a part of the lives of us passers-by. And we, the passers-by, also became parts of the life of this dog, who evidently liked to people-watch.

It finally occurred to me that, as long as this dog had become my favorite, it was about time I started petting her. So I did. Sometimes the dog looked up at me when I petted her, and sometimes she didn't. Sometimes she raised her head to meet my hand when I started to pet her, and sometimes she didn't. But never, ever did she make a sound.

Nancy didn't walk along the alley nearly as often as I did, but on the occasions when she did so and when the silent dog was lying by the gate, Nancy was sure to pet her. Then one day Nancy called me at my office to tell me that when she walked along the alley that morning, she learned that the dog had died. The dog's owners had placed a sign on their back fence that read something like this: "To those of you who loved her—Misae died on April __, 2____, at 4 p.m. of a massive stroke—she was 14-1/2." There were several bunches of flowers by the gate, some perhaps placed there by the dog's owners and the rest by some of the people whom the dog had enjoyed watching during those years. Nancy, a day or two later, became one of those who placed flowers by the gate and also one of those (I'm sure there were others) who was brought to tears by the news of Misae's death.

The last time I saw—and petted—the dog, a couple of days before her death, she seemed to be fine, no different than ever. You never know. For some period of days after the dog's death, I had difficulty repressing a sob or two when I passed her gate. She was somebody else's dog, but she had become a significant part of my life.

Misae had indeed become silent, and I missed her. I knew that my regret would have been much greater if I had not had sense enough, finally, to start petting the dog and thus display more clearly the affection I felt for her.

Chapter 13

Rod and Georgia

Numerous mentions have been made of these important personages, but I'll remind you that Rod was seven years older and Georgia two years younger than I. Accordingly, during our childhood, I had more to do with each of them than they had to do with one another. I shared a room with Rod most of the time and, of course, grew up with Georgia. During most of our adult years, however, Rod and Georgia both lived on the West Coast and had much more contact with one another than either had with me. My contact with them during recent decades could be summarized as consisting of a series of hellos and good-byes.

My specific memories about sharing a room with Rod are skimpy, probably because we were seldom in the room at the same time, except when sleeping. And on many nights I was no doubt already asleep by the time Rod went to bed. However, I do remember a few events that occurred before either of us had gone to sleep. One night we each had a flashlight and chased one another's beams around on the ceiling for a while, until the sandman took over. On another night we decided to see how long we could stay awake and rigged a string that was tied to Rod's hand and then ran over to my bed where the other end was tied to my hand. Our objective, of course, was to provide a means for each of us to keep the other from falling asleep. Pulling strings worked for a time, but the sandman once again prevailed.

When I was eleven years old, Rod went off to college and never really returned to our household. Before his freshman year was over, he enlisted in the army. During his service, Rod was stationed at Indiana University for a time in connection with some type of officers' training program. While there, he played first base on the soldiers' baseball team against a team of college boys. Rod acknowledged to me later that he was probably not much better than the first baseman on the college team (a fellow named Ted Kluszewski).

After the war Rod resumed his college education and married Fran. When I was a freshman in college, Rod was in his last year in the graduate school of business at the same university, and he and Fran lived in an apartment in a nearby town. During that year their first child, Linda (the "walking doll" mentioned earlier), was born, and I became her first babysitter.

In the years following his graduation, Rod held several different jobs in the business world and resided in several different places, in the Chicago area and elsewhere. At about the time when I finished law school and returned to the Chicago area, Rod was also transferred back to that area by the company he worked for. For the next three years or so, we both lived in the northwest suburbs of Chicago and saw one another from time to time. Then he changed jobs, moved to southern California, and lived on the West Coast thereafter.

If I had known that there would be only three years during my adulthood when I would be living near my brother, I suppose I would have arranged to spend more time with him—if he would have stood for it. But during these years I believe I was acting in accordance with what I would call the opportunity theory. This theory states that, although happiness includes the doing of enjoyable things—for example, spending time with one's brother and his family—a more important element of happiness is the opportunity to continue doing enjoyable things in the future and the pleasant prospect which that opportunity presents. I had evidently been thinking along these lines for a few years, for about that time I found an entry, in that little journal referred to earlier in which I jotted things down now and then during my college years, referring to something Jane Austen wrote in one of her books: "that sanguine expectation of happiness which is happiness itself."

Thus, my view, at least subconsciously, was that how much time I spent with Rod and his family was not a critical factor as long as I could look forward to the opportunity of spending time with them on a regular basis in the future. Unfortunately, I got snagged on a corollary to the opportunity theory—namely, the duration of any opportunity is indefinite.

During the years Rod lived on the West Coast, he was, successively, a corporate executive, a partner in a small management consulting firm, a business adviser to an Indian tribe, a financial planner, and, more-or-less, a retiree. He traveled most frequently when he worked for one corporation or another, and we saw him at our place from time to time.

Also, by happenstance, there was one time when we linked up with Rod for a picnic lunch at a lakefront park in Madison, Wisconsin, because he was in that city for a business meeting on the same day we were passing through en route to a vacation stay at Timberlane.

After Rod stopped working for corporations, he traveled less often. During this time, I lived in a western suburb of Chicago for more than ten years and Rod was there only once. On that occasion he was at our home only during hours of darkness, for he arrived from the airport to have dinner with us on a cold winter night and he and I left before dawn the next morning to go back to the airport.

During these years, I also saw Rod on the West Coast from time to time, most memorably when my daughter Pat and I flew out to surprise Rod at his fiftieth birthday party, which Georgia and her husband were hosting at their home in Orange County. Rod's older daughter, Linda, also put in a surprise appearance that night. The evening was made even more special by being the occasion when I met Rod's second wife, Phyllis, who had then been married to him for about a year.

When I was a child, I naturally could not keep up with Rod. I'm sorry to say that I found that this continued to be true during my adult years, and I'll cite one example that shows this pretty clearly. On an occasion when I was at Rod's home in California, I demonstrated something I believe is called a frog squat. In this operation, you place your palms on the floor, bend your legs, swing your body forward, and put your knees on your elbows, so that you're in kind of a crouching position in the air supported by your arms and hands. (Don't ask me why I did this. I've forgotten—and I would probably say that I've forgotten even if I hadn't.) After observing me do my frog squat, Rod, in his sometime "Aw, shucks" manner, said something to the effect that, gosh, he wondered if he could do that. He then proceeded to get down on the floor and do the same thing I had done—except that he supported himself on his fingertips rather than his palms!

In the light of the foregoing and other comeuppances and defeats over the years, I think I once complained to Rod that he never wanted to compete with me except in activities where he was superior to me. I believe he expressed himself as being at a loss to figure out what alternative I had in mind. I'm not sure whether the foregoing conversation actually occurred or whether I imagined that it must have occurred because there were so many times that I thought he would have thus responded if I had made such a complaint.

There was one occasion when I surpassed Rod in connection with classical music, even though I know virtually nothing about music, classical or otherwise. He mentioned to me that his favorite piece of classical music was a Brahms piano concerto, offered to play a recording of the piece, and put a record on his record player.

It was apparent right away that the record being played was a solo piano piece and, thus, not a piano concerto by Brahms or anyone else. I told Rod this and suggested that the piece sounded like something by Debussy. Rod insisted that it was indeed a Brahms piano concerto and displayed the record jacket from which he had removed the disc in question. Although the jacket supported Rod's view, I got ahold of the record itself and pointed out that it confirmed that the piece to which we had been listening was a solo piano piece by Debussy.

A number of years ago, I called Rod on October 17 and asked him if he knew the significance of the date. When he professed ignorance, I reminded him that it was our dad's birthday and, as a matter of fact, his 100th birthday. Rod then described to me something very strange that had happened the same day. It seems that while Phyllis was rummaging around in a dresser drawer, a newspaper clipping that had been at the bottom of the drawer slipped through a crack and fluttered to the floor. This particular clipping was the one that told of our father's death and had of course been saved by Rod for many years. However, when Rod heard from Phyllis about the clipping falling on the floor, it didn't remind him of the significance of October 17, in general, or of that October 17, in particular. It almost seems like Dad was looking on the scene, saw that the newspaper clipping did not trigger Rod's memory, and decided that he better arrange to have "old pill, pal, Paul" call his older brother and give him a reminder.

Earlier I mentioned that Georgia and I grew up together. Unfortunately, for a time I did not grow up fast enough, and she almost caught up to me in height, when I was thirteen or fourteen and she was eleven or twelve. What a disgrace for me! It was at about this time that she and I took a walk downtown one summer day to view the V-J Day celebration in the main town square. Georgia and I walked lots of places together, especially in our younger years. I've already mentioned Sunday school and Georgia's nursery school, and sometimes we walked down the street to the neighborhood grocery store to get a loaf of bread or whatever.

However, the place to which we most often walked together was our grade school. In Georgia's first two or three years of school, it was important for big brother to escort baby sister. A special problem was that, in order to get to our school, we had to cross a U.S. highway at a place where there were no traffic signals. There were patrol boys stationed there, but nevertheless the process of getting safely across that wide and busy street could sometimes be exciting.

The days when I accompanied Georgia on walks to school were the first occasion when I ran into a phenomenon that I have found to be prevalent everywhere and in all situations—it takes a female a much longer time than a male to get ready to go anywhere. In the case of Georgia and me, the long front sidewalk at our house played a role in the Georgia-caused delays in our leaving for school. Our house was located about halfway between the street and the edge of the Old Cem. It was indeed a long way—say, seventy-five feet—down a narrow sidewalk from our house to the street. Evidently our parents owned a very narrow strip of land on which this sidewalk was located, for it was hemmed in on both sides by neighboring houses and yards.

At any rate, my procedure on school mornings, after I had waited for a while inside the house for Georgia to get ready, was to announce to her that I was leaving, walk partway down our front sidewalk, pause, wait, go back, say to Georgia something along the lines of, "Come on, or I'm really leaving," and then repeat the procedure, perhaps walking a little farther down that long front sidewalk each time. I don't believe I ever went off to school without Georgia in these situations, but I know that I waited for her almost every time if not indeed 100 percent of the time.

One of Georgia's functions as a younger sister was to tag along after me from time to time. Earlier I mentioned one instance of this that ended up with my mouth being washed out with soap. Once in a while, on the other hand, I tagged along after Georgia, in a sense, by joining in one of her activities. For example, she was once able to induce me to "pour" at a tea party she put on for a couple of her dollies.

My childhood relationship with Georgia sometimes involved teasing by me and efforts to retaliate physically by her. Though I naturally wasn't worried about what she would do if she caught me, part of the fun was to avoid having her catch me. Thus, from time to time when neither of our parents was home, we became involved in chases through the house, with a furious Georgia pursuing a laughing Paul. A lamp was tipped over once upon a time, and another time Georgia kicked the upstairs bathroom door so hard (after I had taken refuge behind the only lockable door inside the house) that part of the molding fell off the door. I don't recall how that was explained to our parents, but Georgia maintains to this day that I did the door kicking. I hope you know better than to believe her.

Sometimes when Dad reprimanded Georgia and me during the course of our bickering, he would reject our usual excuses (e.g., "She poked me first!" or "He started it!") by means of the time-honored mathematical formulation: "Two wrongs don't make a right." He also advised us on many such occasions that he did not want to hear any "ifs, ands, or buts."

Georgia, being a little sister, was of course a tattletale. I can't begin to remember all of the instances when she tattled to our mother, but I *know* she was a tattletale and suppose that I furnished numerous grounds for tattling. I do vividly remember one such occasion when I was in the seventh grade and for some reason decided to meow like a cat in the schoolroom when the teacher's back was turned. When the teacher figured out who was doing the meowing, she marched me off to the principal's office, where it was decided that I would spend the rest of the day in the first-grade classroom since I had been acting like a first-grader.

It was bad enough to be required to sit on one of those little chairs amongst the first-graders, but I also discovered to my horror that on this particular day the first-graders were putting on some kind of musical performance and that the pupils in the other grades would be coming, one grade at a time, to view the performance in the first-grade room. When the fifth grade, Georgia's grade, arrived, she would also view me, our parents would be informed, and I would be in the soup. The fifth-grade students did eventually arrive, Georgia saw me, and...that's all. As she confirmed to me many years later, she didn't tattle this time. Sweet little sister.

(Years earlier, when I was a first-grader myself, there was another occasion when I was singled out for special treatment in the first-grade room. I had not as yet learned to tie my shoelaces and evidently pestered the teacher by asking her to retie my laces from time to time. At some point she had had enough, sat me down on one of the little chairs at the front of the room, facing my classmates, and told me to stay there until I was able to tie my own shoelaces. Would you believe that all of my children learned to tie their shoelaces long before they started school?)

Have I mentioned that Georgia is more of a go-getter than I? I guess that horse died some pages back, but I will relate a couple incidents from my adulthood that furnish examples of Georgia taking the initiative and that occurred during a trip Georgia, Barbara, and I once took up the California coast from Orange County to Berkeley. One of the places we stopped was the Hearst Castle at San Simeon, which Georgia had previously toured. We had not made reservations ahead of time, but it was off-season, and we were hopeful of being able to take a tour. We were disappointed to learn that no tour tickets were available, but Georgia said she would see what she could do, disappeared for a time, and returned with two tickets. She didn't tell us how she had done it, but I assume she gave the powers that be a sob story about brother and wife coming all the way from Illinois, dying to see the castle, etc.

The next day we had lunch at Fisherman's Wharf in San Francisco. This was at a place where the proprietor operated a market on the ground floor and a restaurant upstairs. We enjoyed a nice lunch, which included part of a loaf of very tasty bread. As I was paying the bill, Georgia asked the waiter to wrap up the remainder of the bread so that we could take it along. He replied that he could not do that but that she could buy another loaf at the market downstairs. The waiter departed, and Georgia said something to the effect of, "The hell with that noise," and stuffed the remaining bread into her handbag. As we walked out of the restaurant, I said to Georgia in a joshing manner that I was embarrassed to be seen in public with her when she behaved like that. Just then I happened to glance down and notice the large red cloth napkin tucked into my pants.

There is one other restaurant incident that occurred years later, which I want to interject here even though neither Georgia nor Rod was involved. The scene was a hotel in a Chicago suburb where Nancy and I had gone to have dinner and see a stage show on a very cold winter night. When we finished dinner, we each decided to make a pit stop before going to the theater on the other side of the hotel, and I decided to wear my overcoat instead of carrying it. I went into the men's room, stood at a urinal, reached for my fly, and (relax—I'm not going to be gross or even try to be salacious) couldn't find my zipper. Surely my pants had a zipper. Of course they did. Surely I hadn't put my pants on backwards. Of course I hadn't. After some semi-desperate fumbling, I finally found my zipper…right there, under the big cloth napkin hanging down from my waist.

Chapter 14

Begging the Question and Other Misusages

According to the Random House Dictionary of the English Language, second edition, unabridged, issued in 1987, "to beg the question" means to assume the truth of the very point raised in a question. For instance, if the issue is whether a certain person ever beat his wife, asking that person when he stopped beating his wife begs the question. No doubt the most well-known instance of question begging is Descartes' "I think, therefore I am."

In the last twenty or so years I have noticed an increasing usage of the phrase "begging the question" as meaning that the circumstances are such that a particular question could or should be asked. I suppose it is possible that a more recent dictionary might indicate that a usage of the type described is no longer unacceptable, but I would be surprised if that is the case.

At some point during the time period referred to I noticed that such a usage of "begs the question" was made by Frasier Crane on the *Frasier* television show. I don't recall the plot of the particular episode and, of course, don't know when it was filmed. The show generally depicted Frasier Crane as being smart, knowledgeable, something of an intellectual bigot, and perhaps one of the last persons you would expect to make such a misusage (assuming that such usage was still unacceptable at the time in question).

A more widespread misusage I have also noticed in the last twenty or so years is the use of "I" instead of "me" in a variety of situations. I suspect that this may represent a reaction to generations of children asking questions such as “Can Jimmy and me go to the movies?” and generations of parents answering, “Don’t say ‘me’—say ‘I.’” Some of those parents might also have said, “Don’t say ‘can’—say ‘may.’”

Just between you and I, I hope that what I just said has not become acceptable.

Chapter 15

Automotive Adventures

The 6,200-Mile Trip

Many years ago, Barbara and I drove with the children from the Chicago area to Orange County, California, to visit my mother, brother, sister, and other relatives. We took the southerly route out, which pretty much followed the path of old U.S. Route 66 and thus in large part retraced (in the opposite direction) my longest hitchhiking trip. On the way back after our visit, we drove up the Pacific coast and didn't turn east until we had reached Bend, Oregon, which I believe is farther from the Chicago area than Orange County is.

Thus, we covered some 6,200 miles with five children in the car, the oldest of whom was ten and all of whom behaved very well throughout the trip. As I expect is the case with most kids, our kids were not real interested in sightseeing while we were traveling. Their main objective was to reach the motel at the end of the day and get in the pool. As it turned out, however, at least on the way back home, there were several nights when we did not reach our lodging place until well after darkness had descended. The reason for this was our failure to make advance reservations for lodging on the return trip. The reason for that, in turn, is that our route for the return trip was determined day by day as we traveled.

One thrill for me on the way out to California was pulling off the road in Oklahoma and spending a few moments watching a pair of scissor-tailed flycatchers sitting on the telephone line above us. This remains the only time I've ever seen such birds. As I wrote this, I was reminded of a similar incident that happened more recently, when Nancy and I and a few others were walking in the woods near the home of friends in central Wisconsin and saw a scarlet tanager fly close to the ground right past us. I hadn't seen that beautiful bird since childhood, and Nancy had never before seen a scarlet tanager. Supposedly little things can sometimes be pretty exciting and memorable.

To return to the days of yesteryear and the 6,200-mile trip: While driving across New Mexico on the interstate, we passed by Clines Corners but didn't stop. I figured I had already put in my quota of time at that location.

One of our stops on the homebound leg of the trip involved a picnic lunch in the mountains near Crater Lake, Oregon, followed by a brief snowball fight. (My only July snowball fight ever.) And Crater Lake was, of course, beautiful. The color of the water was enough to induce Barbara to make the switch to color film for snapshots. (I know that everyone uses color film now, but bear in mind that this trip was a long time ago.)

A couple of days later we were at Yellowstone, where the wildlife seemed to be an even bigger attraction than the geological-type wonders. It appeared that the customary procedure concerning wildlife was to stop whenever you saw other vehicles stopped and to look at whatever the other folks were looking at. In the case of bears congregated in the road, the object of everyone's attention was obvious. However, at another place where we pulled up behind some other cars, it was very difficult to discern what animal was available for viewing. Finally, we were able to spot what seemed to be a lone moose about half a mile away. Whatever thrill was generated by that sight was short lived, for a mile or two down the road there were a half dozen moose within about fifty yards of the highway.

The day after Yellowstone we saw Devil's Tower in northeastern Wyoming. I had been interested in this place from the time when, during my childhood, a picture of it was printed in the newspaper because an airplane had crashed or crash-landed on top of it.

All in all, the 6,200-mile trip is a pleasant memory. Despite the length of the trip, the car full of young kids, and the problems of lining up lodgings each day on the way home, I was not so stressed out as to be tempted to resume the smoking habit that I had finally given up about two months before we set out on the trip.

The Cape Crusader

We stayed at a motel at the west edge of Philadelphia on the Friday night before we reached Cape Cod to fish for eels, as I described in an earlier chapter. At the time, we didn't realize that eel fishing was to be our fate, but we did know that, come hell or high water, we wanted to arrive the next day at the cabin we had rented on Cape Cod.

There were five children along on this trip, too, and by now the oldest was thirteen. With so many people in our station wagon, there wasn't a whole lot of room for luggage, and all of the suitcases, etc., were accordingly transported in a rooftop carrier.

The first stop on our Saturday journey was to be downtown Philadelphia, where we would park the car and take a walking tour to see Independence Hall, Franklin's grave, etc. Because we would be away from the car for an hour or more and because the carrier, though zippable, was not lockable and, in any event, was slashable, we put all of the suitcases, etc., in the car with us while we drove downtown from the motel. This time the kids were glad to get out of the excessively cozy quarters in the car and do a little sightseeing. And after the Philadelphia sightseeing was over, Daddy put all of the suitcases, etc., in the rooftop carrier, and we set out on the next stage of the journey.

Right after we crossed the Delaware River into New Jersey, we arrived at a fork in the freeway and were delighted that we were bound for New York, inasmuch as the alternative, heading toward the Jersey shore, was already jammed with bumper-to-bumper traffic on this beautiful Saturday morning. Similar sights greeted us periodically as we drove north on the New Jersey Turnpike and passed over the Garden State Parkway at various points. The traffic we had seen heading east from Philadelphia to the Jersey shore was more than matched by the miles and miles of standing or crawling traffic bound from the New York area to the Jersey shore on the Garden State Parkway.

We, on the other hand, breezed along toward our lunch destination, the home of a long-time friend who lived in northern New Jersey and worked in Manhattan. After lunch, we headed for New York City and crossed the Hudson through one of the tunnels. We then drove down to the vicinity of Battery Park and parked on the street, for our agenda included taking a look from afar at the Statue of Liberty. (Time didn't permit taking the ferry over to the island for a closer look.) Unfortunately, yours truly got no look at all, due to an unwillingness to leave the car, with that slashable rooftop carrier, alone for even a little while on the streets of New York.

Next was a drive through or past various sites and sights in Manhattan—Herald Square, Empire State Building, Times Square, etc.—as many as we could take in, this being the first time any of the kids had been to New York City. By the time we got out of New York, it was late afternoon, and we still had a long way to go.

I don't remember all the details of the rest of that Saturday. Naturally, we stopped for dinner at some restaurant along the way. And, when we finally reached Cape Cod, I'm sure we had some trouble locating the place where we needed to pick up the keys for our cabin, followed by some trouble locating the cabin itself.

The thing that stands out in my mind concerning the last leg of our trip to Cape Cod was driving over the long, high bridge over Narragansett Bay leading to Newport, Rhode Island. It was, of course, dark by then, and it was also quite foggy. Crossing this bridge under these circumstances was an eerie experience. Because we could see only a short distance ahead, it almost seemed that we were leaving the earth and heading up into space.

The Snowstorm

When I was a senior in high school, our highly rated basketball team participated in a Christmas tournament at Madison, Wisconsin. I went to the tournament with a classmate and friend by the name of Bob and saw our team win both of the games in which it played.

When we headed home thereafter in a car containing other classmates, we found ourselves in the midst of a major blizzard. It was so bad that it became impossible to see anything but snow through the windshield. The driver therefore ended up holding the steering wheel with his right hand, holding the car door open with his left hand, and leaning out into the storm to see as best he could where the hell we were going. Although the description of what the driver was doing may conjure up a rather amusing image, it was, of course, a very serious and dangerous situation. We were luckier than the occupants of the team bus, who were involved in a tragic accident on the way back from Madison, resulting in the death of an assistant coach and injuries to several other players and coaches.

Bob and I have kept in touch since high school days. Each of us has been married, divorced, and remarried. Also, we both have five children, consisting of three older daughters and two younger sons. However, Bob got married and started reproducing at younger ages than I. Years ago we were discussing the rapidity at which Bob's family was growing, and his then wife commented that it seemed that if she was in the bedroom and he walked by the bedroom door, she would get pregnant. My response to her observation was the following question: "Don't you think that's stretching it a bit?"

Drivers' Training

The time when I learned to drive was long before drivers' training courses were available in high schools, and my dad was accordingly my trainer. Our procedure involved my driving along two-lane roads with Dad by my side, instructing and critiquing the while. My main problem seemed to be steering, for he again and again reminded me to keep the hood ornament lined up with the right side of the road.

After I had a number of training sessions but before I had my driver's license, my mother used to let me drive around the neighborhood when I came home for lunch from the high school a few blocks from where we lived. One time when I was doing this, the car conked out as I was driving down the street, but I managed to get it over to the curb as I coasted to a stop. The engine was still running, but the car would not move no matter how hard I pressed on the accelerator. So I abandoned Old Bessy, walked back home, and found out later that the crankshaft had broken.

In later years my kids learned to drive in high school drivers' education courses. Around the time when some of them became licensed drivers, we acquired a stick-shift Vega. Because the school course had made use of automatic transmission vehicles only, it became necessary to provide the kids with some additional drivers' training at one or another empty parking lot in the vicinity. Whenever one of my offspring complained about the difficulties of operating a clutch, it was pointed out that they had it a lot easier than those who, like their father, had been faced with the necessity of learning to deal with a clutch and all of the other aspects of driving at the same time.

Behind Closed and Locked Doors

During the early years of my marriage to Nancy, we went to northwest Indiana to visit some of her relatives and stayed at a motel for a night or two. One morning we were all set to head somewhere and were about to pull out of the parking lot when I realized I had left something I needed in the room. While I was back at the room, Nancy remembered that she had also forgotten something and therefore got out of the car as well. When she did so, she locked the door behind her. And the engine was running.

Nancy had neither a driver's license nor a set of car keys, so our only keys were those in the ignition. A coat hanger would not serve to open the locked door, and we were in a dilemma until we got a police officer to come and unlock the car door with one of those implements that either is or looks like a piece of sheet metal.

The upshot of this incident was that we obtained a set of car keys for Nancy to carry, despite her lack of a driver's license. Also, I had something to razz Nancy about once in a while for a number of years until I suddenly found myself in Nancy's moccasins.

One afternoon during the course of running several errands, I stopped to deliver something to a customer of Nancy's at his shop about a mile from our home. This was on a busy Chicago street with no parking available, so I double-parked. And because I was only going to take a few seconds to make the delivery, I left the engine running. A split second after I shut the door—a split second too late—I realized what I had done.

A very sheepish Paul then called Nancy and ultimately prevailed upon her to bring me the other set of car keys. (I don't recall how often her laughter interrupted my description of the problem and my request for aid.) In case you are wondering why I just didn't go home and get the other set of keys myself, I will explain. Because my double-parked car blocked at least one other car parked at the curb, it seemed judicious to stay at the scene to offer explanations and apologies in case the other driver returned with the intention of driving his or her car elsewhere.

The Glasses and the Car

Over the years, I occasionally used my car to commute to work, on days when I needed to go somewhere besides the office during part of the day. One beautiful spring morning I drove to a north suburb of Chicago to participate in the closing of a real estate transaction. The lawyer representing the other party to the transaction was a fellow by the name of Steve, whom I knew slightly. He lived in the north suburbs, and after the closing I offered to drive him downtown, where our offices happened to be in the same building. Because it was becoming quite warm, we took off our jackets and put them on the back seat.

As we were in the process of disembarking after I parked in a downtown garage, Steve said that he seemed to be missing his glasses, which he had thought were in a jacket pocket. So we made a thorough search of the car, and he made a thorough search of his clothes and briefcase—all to no avail. For some reason (or no reason), I thought that turning the car lights on would aid in the search, for the bright sunshine didn't penetrate very far into this multilevel parking garage.

After we gave up the search and headed for our offices, I remember wondering whether I had turned off the car lights. If I had been alone, I would have gone back to the car to check, but I wanted to avoid the possibility of delaying Steve's arrival at his office and consoled myself with the thought that I would certainly not be so stupid as to leave my lights on in such a situation.

As it happened, I was at the office until quite late that day, and it was after 9 p.m. when I returned to the garage. I was pleased to see that my car lights were indeed not on, but then I was displeased when I got into the car and ascertained the reason why the lights were not on. My next step was to call a tow truck operator to give my battery a jump. I explained to this gentleman that I needed to drive home to the western suburbs and inquired as to whether I would be likely to have trouble getting the car started again if the engine should happen to stall on the way home. The tow truck driver said that could be a problem and strongly recommended that I avoid killing the engine while driving home.

With this warning in mind, I started home and covered the twenty-five or so miles in about two hours, after the engine stopped and had to be restarted several times en route. At the time, I didn't know what the problem was—I just knew that, as I was driving down the freeway, the engine started chugging and lurching in a way that I had never previously experienced and the car quickly lost power. I had to pull over to the shoulder but was able to get the car started again after waiting for a time. I had to repeat this procedure some eight or ten times. Luckily I didn't have any problem getting the engine started each time—the problem was to keep the car going.

As is apparent, the difficulty I ran into while driving home had nothing to do with the battery. It turned out that the source of the problem was a clogged fuel filter. It was evidently just a coincidence that this first interfered with driving on the same day that my battery went dead.

Several weeks later, I noticed a pair of glasses sitting on the kitchen counter. In response to my inquiry, my wife told me that she had come across these glasses in the car. I don't recall how she happened upon the glasses without looking for them when Steve and I had come up empty after our "thorough" search. What I do recall is that, when I was told that the glasses had been in our car, the name Steve reverberated again and again through my brain.

The "Oil Change"

At some point during my adulthood, I decided that it was time for me to save money by doing some of my own automobile maintenance, such as changing the oil and oil filter and rotating the tires. I knew that other guys did that sort of thing, and one thing that prompted me to emulate them in this respect was my awareness that my next-door neighbor had a set of blocks that I could use to raise my car so that I could get under there and drain the oil.

The first time I changed the oil in my car (God, I *hope* it was the first time), I drained the oil and put the plug back in the pan. So far, so good, I thought. The next step was to remove and replace the oil filter, making use of the special oil filter wrench that I had obtained. To my surprise (but, somehow, not to my enlightenment), oil came pouring out when I removed the filter. I don't remember now what I thought was the cause of this deluge, but I managed to clean up the mess and get the new filter on anyway. I then proceeded to put in what I believed was the proper quantity of new oil and concluded that the job was done.

However, when I went to take the car off the blocks and put it away in the garage, I had some problems getting into and out of reverse gear. One thing then led to another, and I finally figured out what you have probably known from the start: I had violated the cardinal rule of oil changes—that the first step is to drain the old oil, not the transmission fluid. Thus, in the case of auto maintenance, just as in the case of golf and fishing, anything other guys can do I can do worser.

My performance in this oil-changing farce would no doubt be a strong candidate for the dumbest thing I ever did if I had not walked in front of Sonny at the edge of the dump so many years before.

Chapter 16

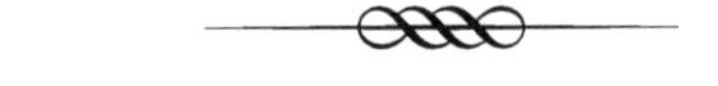

Travels (and Travails) in the Pacific Northwest

My first traveling in the Pacific Northwest occurred during the 6,200-mile trip I talked about earlier. Since that trip I have been out that way quite a few times, largely because Rod lived in that area for many years. I don't intend to describe all of my trips to the Pacific Northwest, but three of them may be of interest from a logistical, a meteorological, or an ecological standpoint.

Logistical

Years ago, in connection with a lawsuit I was working on, I needed to go to Palo Alto, California, to take a witness deposition. At that time my mother and Georgia lived in Orange County, California, and Rod lived on Lopez Island, Washington. Lopez is one of the San Juan Islands located in Puget Sound.

Also at that time, probably due to an airline fare war, it would have been more economical for me to fly from Chicago to Los Angeles and then to San Francisco instead of flying directly to San Francisco. In view of the foregoing and in view of the fact that I very seldom saw my mother, I decided that I would fly to L.A. on Saturday, spend the weekend with my mother, and then fly to San Francisco on Monday in time to reach Palo Alto for the 1 p.m. deposition.

When I tried to call Mom to tell her I would be coming to visit her, I was unable to reach her and then learned, through a call to Georgia, that Mom was up visiting Rod and Phyllis on Lopez Island. Although the economics were no longer the same, obviously it seemed advisable that I visit my mother in Washington on my way to Palo Alto. So I arranged to fly from Chicago to Lopez Island on Saturday. The unusual part of this trip was the nature of the airfields where we landed in the course of the commuter airline trip from Seattle to Lopez. At my destination the airport had a crushed stone runway, but on the way there we landed on a meadow at Port Townsend, Washington. A grass runway!

It later occurred to me that I had previously taken off from and landed on grass when I was a little boy and flew for the first time in an airplane. This was with a barnstormer by the name of Chamberlain, who went around to various towns, arranged to rent a suitable pasture or meadow from a local farmer, and then (for a price) offered to take townspeople on sightseeing flights over their town. A pal of mine who lived across the street was going to take one of these flights with his father, who offered to take me along. I remember that when I returned home after the flight, I found my grandmother in the backyard, waving her handkerchief at Chamberlain's plane flying overhead. I greeted her and asked who she was waving to. She was a little surprised to see me and perhaps also surprised that I didn't figure out who she thought she was waving to.

Rod and Phyllis had a beautiful place on Lopez. The house was situated on high ground from which you could see, through a break in the trees, the bay down below. You could also look over to the mainland and see snow-capped Mount Baker.

The logistical problem I've been leading up to was how to get from Lopez Island to Palo Alto by 1 p.m. on Monday. More particularly, the problem was to get from Lopez to the Seattle-Tacoma airport in time to make the flight I needed to take to San Francisco.

As it worked out, we needed to get up before dawn on Monday morning in order to arrive early enough to be sure of having a spot on the first ferry to Anacortes. We accomplished this and then had to drive at a rather rapid pace to Oak Harbor airport on Whidbey Island, which (thank goodness) is an island of the type reachable by bridge. We arrived in time for me to make the commuter flight to Seattle and connect with my flight to San Francisco.

Meteorological

The journey that had significant meteorological aspects was one taken by Nancy and me in the mid-1980s to spend the New Year holiday with Rod and Phyllis. At that time, they lived on Guemes Island, Washington, which is another of the San Juan Islands but is only about a half mile offshore from Anacortes and is served by a separate ferry that runs to and from Anacortes several times a day. On our way to Guemes, Nancy and I were going to spend a couple of days at Victoria, British Columbia, inasmuch as we had heard that it is a very beautiful and interesting city.

When we left Chicago in late December, the temperature at O'Hare Field was in the low 60s, but when we arrived at Calgary via Air Canada, it was 20 below zero. We took this in stride—we, of course, remained indoors. Although I have applied the meteorological label to this trip, the trip was not without its own logistical problems. (And I guess we all know that meteorological and logistical problems often go hand in hand.)

The Calgary airport was the scene of a logistical problem on this occasion, in that the length of the lineup for clearing Canadian customs was such that we didn't have a chance of getting through customs in time to make our scheduled flight from Calgary to Vancouver, British Columbia. The airline people interceded with the customs people on behalf of us and the few other people who had come in from Chicago and intended to fly on from Calgary to another destination. The customs people initially insisted that we get in line just like regular people, but the airline representatives evidently talked to someone higher up and ultimately got us through customs quickly so that we could get on our Vancouver flight.

However, there was some delay in that flight, either in leaving Calgary or en route, with the result that we reached Vancouver too late to make our scheduled flight to Victoria. Also, it was snowing like mad when we arrived in Vancouver. The airline people directed us to another flight, on a different airline, which was leaving for Victoria shortly from a gate some distance away. We needed to hustle to make this flight, and I remember Nancy turning to me and asking a most appropriate question as we ran through the airport together: "When is it going to start being fun?"

We did get on the flight we were running to catch and then flew from Vancouver across the water to Victoria through a raging snowstorm.

The plane was rather a small one, and this was probably the most nearly thrilling flight I've ever been on. When we landed, there was about a foot of snow on the ground. That part of the world doesn't get much snow at all, and we learned later that we had flown through the biggest blizzard in some twenty years. The airport is located about ten miles from the city of Victoria, and airline passengers are usually taken into the city by a shuttle bus. But we didn't make the shuttle bus—it seemed there was some problem about locating our luggage. (Obviously, it had not started being fun yet.)

Ultimately, we concluded that our luggage was lost, at least for that night, and took a taxi into the city. Seeing the many trees along the way heavily festooned with snow, for one of the few times during their existence, was probably the highlight of our day. Another plus, for me, was the fact that the driving along the snow-covered road was being done by someone else.

We managed to enjoy our short stay in Victoria despite the weather—especially after our luggage finally caught up with us shortly before we left Victoria to take the ferry over to Anacortes. I guess Victoria is a pretty town, but it seems to me that all cities look just about alike at ground level when buried under a foot of snow.

Ecological

Our next trip to visit Rod and Phyllis on Guemes Island occurred during warm weather and resulted in my becoming more deeply involved with tent caterpillars than I had ever dreamed was possible.

The home where our hosts lived on Guemes was, of course, rural, given that all of Guemes was rural. Although no other house was visible from where they lived, plenty of trees and other environment were visible, and you could often see eagles overhead. Rod and Phyllis were very much into organic and do-it-yourself foods and had a very large vegetable garden and a lot of berry bushes.

At the time of this visit, Guemes was subject to a major onslaught of some form of tent caterpillar. Tents and caterpillars were everywhere, including all of the vegetable garden and berry bushes. The Gabler house was also under attack, with caterpillars crawling up and down the outside walls and around the doorways and windows.

Rod was enough of an organic farmer and environmentalist that he was unwilling to use an insecticide to kill the caterpillars. However, he wouldn't go so far as to leave the caterpillars alone to consume all of the plant life that he and Phyllis had worked so hard to grow. So, if you want to kill tent caterpillars without spraying them and thus damaging the environment in other respects, what do you do? Why, of course, you squeeze them, one by one, between thumb and forefinger. Icky goo!

So, during the three or four days of our visit, I spent most of the daylight hours (as did Rod) picking and squeezing caterpillars. How I spent my summer vacation. Or, things to do on Guemes Island when you're alive.

Nancy and I were finally able to tear ourselves away from Guemes and head back home. Our flight had been in the air an hour or so when I happened to notice something crawling up my pants leg. You get just one guess as to what it was.

Chapter 17

Some Waterfalls I Have Known and Other Favorite Places

I love waterfalls and have a hunch that this feeling makes me a member of a very large group of people. For someone doing a little writing about waterfalls, a good place to start is Yosemite. In the mid-1980s, Nancy and I made our only trip to Yosemite and spent a couple of days there in early November with Georgia and her second husband, Ray. On the first day, we left our cabins at Currie Village in Yosemite Valley and took a drive of about twenty miles, which, after we stopped to do some hiking along the way, ultimately brought us to a place called Glacier Point. This was about 3,000 feet directly above our cabins and has the deserved reputation of presenting one of the greatest vistas on earth. We stood at Glacier Point for quite some time, enjoying the views of waterfalls, cliffs, mountains, and sky.

Our plans for the next day were to do some lengthy hiking to and around one or more waterfalls. However, Mother Nature thwarted us during the night, when more than a foot of snow fell on Yosemite Valley. It's not smart or permissible for people (or, at least, novices like us) to hike at Yosemite when there is snow on the trails and everywhere else. The next day we did drive to the foot of Yosemite Falls but could see only the lower falls. The upper falls, shrouded in mist, fog, etc., were completely invisible.

We had originally come into Yosemite Valley from the west, via a tunnel through a mountain. In this respect, I regard Pittsburgh as something of a man-made Yosemite. That is, coming out of the tunnel on the freeway leading from the airport to downtown Pittsburgh and seeing the rivers, bridges, and skyscrapers of the Golden Triangle spread out below is, to me, reminiscent of exiting the tunnel through the mountain at Yosemite and finding El Capitan and some of the other splendors suddenly revealed before you.

In times prior to the visit to Yosemite, family vacations often included waterfall viewing. This probably began when we were at Yellowstone during the 6,200-mile trip. However, only Pat accompanied me on the walk down to the brink of the Lower Yellowstone Falls, along one of those walkways that double back and forth down the side of a steep hill. The falls were certainly worth seeing, and I expect that a larger group would have gone down to see them if it had not entailed a long walk back up the hill afterwards.

On a couple of other trips, we stopped briefly at Niagara Falls, and on another vacation, we saw a number of waterfalls in western North Carolina, which (we were told) has the greatest concentration of waterfalls in the U.S.A. In the case of one of these waterfalls, we had to drive about ten miles off the highway on an unpaved road in order to arrive at the vantage point from which the falls could be viewed. When we arrived, the waterfall seemed still to be about a half mile away, and some of it was blocked from even our long-range view by the intervening forest. Our destination had turned out to be more of a "disadvantage" point, and that whole experience was a bummer.

Naturally, we preferred to visit waterfalls we could get close to, and Fall Creek Falls in Tennessee, therefore, interested us when we learned that it was possible to walk behind the waterfall itself. When we arrived at the state park where the falls were located, we found that to reach the base of the falls we would need to clamber about 200 feet down quite a steep slope. While Barbara remained above, from where the waterfall could be seen from a distance, the five kids (who then ranged in age from seven to fourteen) and I made our way down past trees, thickets, and other undergrowth to the bottom of the steep slope. My memory is that, in doing so, we were traveling cross-country (or more accurately, down-country) rather than on a trail. But I don't recall whether this was because there was no trail or because I failed to locate the trail or because the trail was so overgrown that there seemed to be no trail at all.

On reaching the bottom of the little canyon that Fall Creek Falls had created, we did indeed hike over to the waterfall and spend a few minutes walking around behind the curtain of water. While we were down there, I looked up and saw a woman in an orange blouse standing at the top of the cliff and looking down in our direction. Though I couldn't make out her face at that distance, I waved to her and told the children to wave to their mother. Of course, when we got back up to the top I saw that Barbara was wearing something other than an orange blouse. I've never been good at keeping in mind what attire a wife of mine is wearing. As to the kids, I don't know whether they suffered from a similar infirmity or whether they were just so obedient that, on my direction, they would wave to a woman who was not their mother.

A couple of years previously, our vacation itinerary included Crabtree Falls in the Blue Ridge Mountains of Virginia. Unlike the cataracts of Niagara, Yosemite, and Fall Creek Falls, Crabtree is a cascade formed by a creek that comes bouncing down a mountainside. When we visited Crabtree, Barbara and our youngest, Tom, stayed in the car while the rest of us did a little hiking. We walked up alongside Crabtree Creek for a ways and then walked across the creek on rocks at one or two places. We could see that the cascade extended quite a distance up the mountain from where we were, but we spent probably less than half an hour hiking at Crabtree and didn't go very far up the hill because Barbara and Tom were sitting in the car beside the road in an area that was pretty much out in the middle of nowhere.

About fifteen years later, Nancy and I went to Crabtree Falls and found everything changed. Now there was a parking lot, a trail, fences, and other barricades and various warning signs commanding visitors to stay on the trail and stressing how slippery and dangerous it was around the creek and adjacent rocks. During that fifteen-year period, Big Brother had apparently become much more concerned about the safety and welfare of the public or, perhaps, had more tax money in hand that had been allocated for such purposes. In any event, Nancy and I stayed on the trail, went all the way to the top of the falls, and enjoyed Crabtree Falls very much.

Somewhere along the line, Nancy and I also spent a day or two hiking at Starved Rock State Park in Illinois, with Nancy's brother, Phil, and a friend of theirs. The hiking venues at Starved Rock included about eight or ten little canyons, or glens. We hiked into each of these and, to our delight, found that there was a small cataract-type waterfall at the head of each canyon.

Nancy and I also visited the big cataract, Niagara. Again, this occurred quite a few years after I had gone to Niagara during my prior incarnation. We stayed for several days in a hotel on the Ontario side, within walking distance of the falls. On the night we arrived, we walked down to the falls at about 11 p.m. Nancy had never been to Niagara, so we wanted to see the falls right away. When we had walked to within a couple of blocks of the falls, Nancy commented that it had started to rain. She felt better about the situation when I assured her that what she was feeling was not rain but spray from the falls.

We did a lot of the touristy things at Niagara and enjoyed them, though we had mixed feelings about that goose-drownder boat trip to the foot of the Canadian falls. We also spent some time on Goat Island, the island in the middle of the river where you can get quite close to both the Canadian and American falls. One day, as we stood on the island and watched the waters of the Niagara River race past us toward the American falls, I gave forth with a string of comments that one drop of water in the river might have made to his neighboring drops of water as they all sped along at an accelerating rate. I can't now reconstruct the monologue exactly, but it went something like this: "Hey, fellows, we're really starting to move faster, aren't we? No need for you guys behind me to start shoving, though. I would really prefer not to go this fast. Could we slow it down, please? Hey, quit pushing back there. Omigosh, we're coming to the edge of something. Aieeeee!"

In addition to waterfalls, I'm very partial to the seashore. There are very few things I like better than sitting on a motel balcony, reading a book, and listening to (and often glancing at) the surf. When Nancy and I walk on an ocean beach, we like to stand close to the water and then pretend to flee for our lives as each wave rolls up the beach. We also like to watch the sandpipers scurrying about and likewise pretending to flee for their lives. Our regret is that our seashore visits have been few and far between.

A number of years ago, we visited Rod and Phyllis at their home on a bluff overlooking the Oregon seashore. What a view! Rod told us that, from time to time, he could look out a window and see a whale breaching.

Each day Nancy and I made sure we went down to the beach, where a couple of times we saw a seal or two romping in the surf. A portion of the shoreline consisted of an enormous rock pile, the lower parts of which were the scene of lots of crashing surf. Here our game was to dare each breaker by standing near the edge of the rocks and then jumping back as far as necessary in order to avoid a drenching, at the same time hoping to avoid also any misstep on a slippery rock.

The effect of high tide is another feature of the seashore that I find fascinating, whether the tide covers the entire beach at Daytona Beach, Florida; eliminates an entire peninsula of land at Ogunquit, Maine; or does something else somewhere else.

From my limited experience and knowledge, my impression is that, compared to the West Coast, the East Coast is virtually lined with hotels and motels right on the beach. I suppose there are cultural, historic, governmental, topographical, and other reasons for this state of affairs, but from a touristy point of view, it's a shame. A west-facing balcony on a West Coast beachfront motel would be great for sunset viewing.

Most of the seashore traveling that Nancy and I have done has been in California, and we once found what we were looking for—a motel right on the beach. As we drove north along California Highway 1 overlooking a small town, we noticed a long pier and decided to go down and take a look. Shortly thereafter, while standing on the pier, we spotted a nearby motel right on the beach! We went over and checked in, and since then we have gone back to the same motel in the same little California town a couple of other times. There's not much to do in that little town unless, like us, you enjoy walking on the beach, sitting on a balcony and reading and watching the surf, and then strolling to one or another nearby restaurant for dinner. The first couple of times we stayed at that motel there was a creek bed right next to it, which during some parts of the year evidently carried water into the Pacific. The added attraction created for us by the creek bed was the croaking of the gazillions of frogs that inhabited it and serenaded us every night.

On another trip, when we were southbound on California 1, we again sought a motel on the beach. On the map I noticed a highway running west from Lompoc to the sea and then, apparently, running along the ocean for some distance. Could that highway along the ocean be lined by a string of motels on the beach, or at least one? Although it was a long shot, we decided to check it out. What we found alongside that coastal highway was anything but a group of beachfront motels—it was a railroad yard!

In addition to motel balconies overlooking the ocean surf, I favor other locations where I can sit and read a book. On a long-ago vacation, I spent a good deal of time on the balcony of a chalet on the side of a little mountain in the middle of Asheville, North Carolina. This was so pleasurable that I even remember the book I was then reading: Thackeray's *Pendennis*. And when I lifted my eyes from the book I could look down through the trees at the valley below.

The front stoop of my house in Elgin became a favorite spot for a brief time one summer morning before dawn. I have no memory as to why I was up at that hour, but I went out to see whether the milk had already been delivered. I happened to look up and saw above me, in the southeastern sky, Sirius, Orion, and the other bright stars and constellations that occupy that part of the sky on winter evenings. Although I knew that these winter stars are also visible during the wee hours of summer mornings, I did not have this in mind at the time and was really awestruck by the spectacle, which was made even more spectacular by the fact that Jupiter was sitting up there amongst those stars.

Chapter 18

An Epitome Epiphany and Other Blind Spots

From the time when I was a child, I've been aware of a word pronounced "i-pit'-uh-mē" and meaning a typical or an ideal example. Although, as far as I knew, I had never seen the word in print, I had heard it spoken from time to time. I *had* seen in print, on occasion, a word spelled "e-p-i-t-o-m-e" and pronounced, I assumed, "é-pi-tōm."

Sometime when I was about the age of forty, I again happened to see the word "epitome" in something I was reading, and it occurred to me that "epitome" has the same meaning as "i-pit'-uh-mē." An instant later, I realized, "Oh, my God, it *is* 'i-pit'-uh-mē.'"

There are other words that I believe are more commonly mispronounced than "epitome"—for example, "solder" and "victuals." Two others that I had problems with when I was a child are "colonel" and "rendezvous," but only in the case of "epitome" did it take me anything like forty years to recognize my mistake.

I ran into a somewhat similar problem when the local zoo out at Lord's Park acquired a lion and a contest was conducted to pick a name for him. Subsequently it was announced in the newspaper that the name selected was Lord Spark. Although I thus saw the lion's name in print, I never heard anyone pronounce it and I missed the obvious connection until someone happened to mention it to me. Then the embarrassment set in.

I guess that I can try to console myself with the thought that my failure to connect Lord's Park and Lord Spark at least tends to demonstrate that I don't sound out words when I read.

The difficulty I have thus had a cup love times in coordinating the sights, sounds, and meanings of certain words has sometimes made it difficult for me to beacon tent and to tree chew nice, especially when it is coal doubt.

In connection with the sound of words, I had an apparent difference of opinion years ago with Susan, one of the other attorneys at the law firm where I worked, concerning the pronunciation of the letters "ch" at the beginning of a word. She contended that those letters could not be pronounced as "sh" at the beginning of any word. I couldn't believe she was serious but went along with the gag, so to speak, and gave her a "brief" supporting my view, a copy of which is included as Appendix B.

Chapter 19

Collaterals

My father was one of eleven children and my mother was one of eight, so I had a lot of collateral relatives. I assume you understand that "collateral relative" does not refer to a relative who will co-sign a note for you. I don't have any such relatives, but in addition to all those aunts and uncles, I had thirty-seven first cousins and would have had more if some of my aunts and uncles hadn't been childless. You may think that one of my first cousins was the namesake of a prominent movie actor; but my cousin, Clark Gabler, was born years before there was an actor with a similar name.

When I was a child, I knew and had contacts with many (though certainly not all) of my aunts, uncles, and cousins, particularly because a number of them lived in Elgin. Of course, it was much more common in those days than now for a person to live and die in the same town where he or she had been born. My children have nowhere near as many cousins as I had, and, when my kids were young, their cousins lived very far away from where we lived. So my children basically missed out on those cousin-cousin relationships that often can be close and happy. Tom got a demonstration of this when, during his teen years, he and his mother and I went to Orange, California, to spend Thanksgiving weekend with Georgia and her family. I think Tom was surprised and extremely delighted by the cordiality with which he was greeted and entertained by Georgia's children, especially by her youngest daughter, who is closest to Tom in age.

As for my collaterals, I know I couldn't even list them all from memory, and I sure don't intend to make an effort here to say something about each and every one of them. However, I hope to say something of interest about a few of them.

Because I believe in ladies first, I'll start with my cousin Patty Dailey, a daughter of one of my mother's sisters. Pat was about four years older than I and was in her last semester of high school when I was in my first semester. I have the impression that she was rather wild in those days, and I know that she sported a Mohawk haircut for at least part of her senior year.

During the bus trip to California that I later took with Pat, she started calling me Odd Pod. The "Odd" part is, of course, easy to figure out, and though I know of no reason for "Pod," there was at least rhyme. When I returned to Illinois that summer, Pat stayed in California; and thereafter we saw each other on very infrequent occasions.

When a family vacation took us westward many years later (the 6,200-mile trip), we drove over to where Pat lived in the Los Angeles area. Upon arriving there, I saw her standing on the sidewalk across the street from her home, talking to a neighbor, and got out of the car and walked toward her. Because I was looking at her, she asked if I wanted to talk to her. As it was apparent that she didn't recognize me, I announced: "I'm Odd Pod." Then, of course, she was all over me with oohs, aahs, hugs, etc.

Patty served as a babysitter for Georgia and me on one occasion that I remember. She spent part of the time teaching us how to belch at will, a skill (?) that I retain to this day. Georgia is noncommittal as to whether she still has this ability.

When I was about thirteen years old, I ran into a problem when I was home alone doing the dishes one day. (Talk about weird: a thirteen-year-old boy home alone washing dishes!) I've got to believe I had been instructed to do so. At any rate, it seems that because a particular drinking glass was cracked or because the dishwater was especially hot, or both, a kind of V-shaped piece of glass broke off at the rim of this tumbler when it was in the dishwater. When I thrust the dishcloth into the tumbler in order to wash the inside of it, the knuckle at the base of my index finger fit right into the notch created in the rim of the tumbler where the piece of glass had broken off. I didn't feel a thing and, because this happened while my hands and the tumbler were under water, I was unaware of the problem until I saw the dishwater turning red.

Now I became aware that there was a crisis, and now it would be determined whether I was the man (or boy) to face that crisis. Did I staunch the flow of blood with the dish towel that was within easy reach in the kitchen? Why, hell no! I ran upstairs to my room, spattering blood on carpet and wallpaper along the way, and tried to get a bandage out of my handy-dandy Boy Scout first-aid kit. While I was struggling to open the cellophane-wrapped package containing the bandage, the phone rang. Did I, knowing I was in the midst of a crisis, ignore the phone and concentrate on getting that damn bandage out of the package and onto my knuckle? Why, hell no! I went to answer the phone. And who was the telephone call from? Good ol' cousin Pat. At that time she lived only a block away, so as soon as I told her what had happened, she came right over and we went downtown to a doctor's office and got my knuckle stitched up.

A relative on my father's side with whom I had quite a bit of contact over the years was his older sister Margaret. My dad was quite close to Aunt Margaret, partly because the two of them were on the same side in some family dispute, which I never understood, relating to "the estate." At any rate, from time to time Dad would go over to Margaret's house, taking me with him, and the two of them would sit and talk…and talk…and talk. I don't recall what they talked about (probably "the estate"…and cabbages and kings), and I may never have known, inasmuch as I paid little attention to what they were saying.

Aunt Margaret and her husband, Art, owned a cabin at a lake in northwestern Wisconsin, and our family spent a vacation there one summer. My principal memories about this trip are that Rod hogged the inner tube whenever we went swimming or wading in the lake and that the bathroom facilities were not located in the cabin. This probably was where I first became acquainted with the additional use for a Sears Roebuck catalog.

Despite the nature of my youthful relationship with Aunt Margaret, during my adult years I visited her many times at her home and, finally, at a nursing home. She survived my dad for decades, survived Art for many years, and lived to a ripe old age, dying when she was ninety-eight or thereabouts. Right up to the end she was feisty, interesting, and fun. On many of these visits, I was accompanied by some of my children, and in later years, Nancy went with me. I know that Nancy, as well as I, much enjoyed visiting Margaret; I believe that my kids enjoyed her also. I don't believe any of the kids reacted to a visit to Margaret as I had reacted during my childhood, but of course my adult visits to her did not last nearly as long as those of my childhood and the conversational topics were, I feel sure, less serious than the matters that my dad and Margaret had discussed years earlier. And, of course, I could be wrong in my reading of my kids' feelings concerning a visit to Aunt Margaret.

During one of the visits Nancy and I made to Margaret in the last years of her life, when she was in a nursing home, I asked Margaret whether her father was Jewish, and during another visit, I let Margaret look at some photographs that I had brought along, which she then seemed reluctant to give back to me. I will provide some background concerning both of these matters.

The inquiry as to the possible Judaism of my grandfather stemmed from a phone call I had received from Rod. He said our mother had mentioned to him at some point that her father-in-law was Jewish, and he went on to say that this was naturally of interest to him because his second wife, Phyllis, is Jewish. Because Aunt Margaret was the only surviving member of her generation of the family with whom either of us was in contact, Rod asked me to inquire about her father's religious persuasion when I next visited her. I said that I would be glad to ask the question but that I didn't expect to find that he was Jewish, inasmuch as he was buried in a Catholic cemetery.

When I did ask Margaret whether her father was Jewish, her immediate response was, "No. Polish." I recognize, though Margaret may not have recognized, that it is possible to be both Jewish and Polish. I couldn't care less whether my grandfather was Jewish, Polish, German, or whatever, but I have a hunch that, with a name like Gabler, he was of German extraction and was referred to by Margaret as being Polish because he came from Posen (Poznan). Based on a general knowledge of history rather than any particular research, I believe that that city has had, over the centuries, a mix of Polish and German inhabitants (some of whom were Jewish), has been in the country of Poland most of the time as it is now, and was, at the time of my grandfather's birth, part of Prussia.

Now for some background regarding those photographs I mentioned. Their source was my cousin, Nancy, the youngest child of Uncle Joe.

After her mother's death during the 1980s, Nancy, in the course of going through her mother's effects, came across a photo album containing many very old photographs of her father's family. She called me to let me know that she had some old pictures of my father, which she expected I would like to see, and we arranged to get together for that purpose. I was keenly interested in seeing any such pictures because the earliest photograph of my father that I had ever seen was a head shot taken when he was in the army during World War I. (Although my dad was lucky enough not to see action, my understanding is that he was in France and about to board a train for the front when the Armistice was declared.)

The photo album that my cousin Nancy had found proved to be a treasure trove, and five of the pictures were of special interest to me. There were two head shots of my dad, one taken when he was in the army and the other probably a year or so earlier. The other three photos showed my grandmother with her three daughters; the eight Gabler brothers, probably in 1917, inasmuch as my dad was in an army uniform and his younger brother Tom in a navy uniform; and the entire family except for the oldest son, Louis, probably in 1906, inasmuch as the youngest child was a babe in arms. This last photograph was the most thrilling to me because it showed my dad as a boy of eleven. Nancy arranged to have three sets of these photos made, one for me, one that I sent to Rod, and one that I handed to Georgia in person on a later occasion. I remember that Georgia's reaction on first seeing these photographs of our dad was similar to what mine had been—the tears flowed.

The next time my wife Nancy and I visited Aunt Margaret, we took along the photo album in which we had placed the five old photographs. Margaret was also moved upon seeing these pictures. It took her back—way back. After looking at the photos, Margaret pretended to hide the album by putting it behind her in the chair and then pretended that she would not return it to us. She really did like those old photographs, and she really remained a great kidder to the end.

Those pictures of my dad and his family also reminded me that you are who you are no matter how old you are. This was particularly brought home to me in connection with my uncle Frank, my father's next older brother. Frank was one of the few in my father's siblings who, during my childhood, did not live in Elgin. He always lived far away from where I lived and has been dead for many years, though he survived my father for quite some time. I saw him very infrequently but did correspond with him for a time in my adult years. I remember in one letter how Frank expressed his great sadness at having lost his brother George (my dad) years earlier and how he wished he could be with his brother again. As it happened, Frank's death occurred not very long after he wrote me this letter. When, years later, I saw in the 1906 photograph the thirteen-year-old Frank standing with eleven-year-old George, it was easier to understand the emotions Frank had expressed in that letter to me.

Once in a while during my adult years, I visited a couple of my dad's brothers from whom he had been estranged during the latter years of his life, evidently because of the dispute about "the estate." Sometimes one or more of my children accompanied me on these visits, and at the home of one of my uncles a box of toys was always available for the kids. My impression is that these toys had been around that house since the childhood of my uncle's own offspring. Perhaps many families include oldsters who have toys on hand for the use of visiting members of the youngest generation.

You may recall two of my mother's younger brothers, Howard and Bob, as being gas station operators during some period of time. It is my understanding that years earlier, during the Depression, each of them rode the rails to and from California on one or more occasions. Howard ended up settling on the West Coast but spent the war years in the army. After the war, I (like many other young American boys) received a few military souvenirs, and during the war Howard sent me a box of K rations a couple of times. I was aware that GIs regarded K rations with disdain, but I enjoyed munching on those big hunks of solid chocolate included in the K rations. Also during the war, Aunt Dorothy and her family acquired a dog, which they named Corpy, in honor of Howard, who was a corporal at the time.

What I have always regarded as my earliest memory is associated with Uncle Howard. I was two years and some months old when Georgia was born, and I have a memory that Howard took me on a streetcar to visit Mom and newborn Georgia in the hospital. As is the case with such things, however, I may not actually remember the event but instead remember people telling me that Howard took me on such a visit.

As the photo in Appendix A indicates, Howard and I had dealings even before I was two. Rod is looking up at me and probably wondering how his baby brother got to be so fat, and it's apparent why Uncle Howard called me Puddin' Pud in those days.

After World War II, Howard married and settled in the Phoenix area, where he and his wife resided for many years. I visited them there on the few occasions over the years when I have been in that area. One of these occasions was in late April 1983, when Nancy and I stopped in Phoenix on our way to Orange County, California, to attend the wedding of Georgia's older son. Howard was also going to the wedding, and he provided us a memorable drive over to California. Memorable because, at that time of the year, the desert is in bloom and is especially beautiful and also because Howard was a great conversationalist on a variety of subjects—for example, the desert plants, the geography of the area, and his work during his youth on the construction of the aqueduct to Los Angeles. In addition, we stopped at one of the towns in the Palm Springs area where Howard introduced us to a great delicacy, a date milkshake!

Uncle Howard was about thirteen years younger than my mother and lived several hundred miles away from where she lived in southern California for many years. During all of those years I lived back east (i.e., in Illinois) and was not aware of the details of the contacts they had with one another. However, I do know that Howard kept in frequent touch with her, arranged for her to visit at his home from time to time, and all in all was a terrific younger brother.

When Nancy and I were in California for the wedding in 1983, we saw my mom and Howard and a number of other relatives one evening at a family gathering at Georgia's house. During the evening, my mother and Howard had a discussion that became rather heated, at least on Mom's side, and that, to the rest of us, was rather hilarious. Howard brought up the subject of when my parents had moved into a particular house back in Elgin and soon found that Mom's memory on the point differed from his. As often happens in such situations, each participant kept reiterating his or her view of the circumstances. My mother also became increasingly impatient with Howard's efforts to convince her that she did not know when she moved into her home. Sometimes they would talk for a bit about a different aspect of the old days, but each time Howard (to the accompaniment of groans from some of the others present) would resume his effort to persuade Mom that her recollection was erroneous. Maybe this was one of those occasions when you had to be there, but to a number of us onlookers (albeit certainly not to the participants), it seemed that we were witnessing a very funny comedy routine.

When we passed through Palm Springs on the way to the wedding, Nancy and I became intrigued with the tram that runs from the valley floor to the top of one of the mountains. A few days later, after the wedding, Georgia's younger son drove us back over to Palm Springs and the two of us took a ride on this tram. Although it was a pleasant day, temperature wise, even on top of the mountain, there was still plenty of snow up there. During the trip up and back down and during the brief time up on top, Nancy took about forty-five snapshots. She apparently thought that it was important to photograph each rock formation, etc., from a variety of angles and perspectives.

There is one other of my collateral relatives that I'll mention again here: my sometime chess opponent, Uncle Joe. During several years after my father's death, I was away from the Chicago area most of the time, finishing college and going to law school. After I returned to the area and started working in Chicago, I saw Joe occasionally. As it turned out, he died about three years later. During those years before his death, we played chess from time to time and also went to high school basketball games together once in a while. At some point during this time period, I adopted the practice, when I called his home, of making the following statement to whomever answered the phone: "I was told to call this number and ask for Joe."

Chapter 20

Odd Pod's Odd Jobs

In the days of yore before I became a lawyer, I held a variety of jobs from time to time, some of which may qualify as odd for one reason or another.

My first job, when I was about ten years old, was working after school at a very small farm operated by the parents of a schoolmate of mine and located at the edge of town. This went on only for a week or two, and I don't remember why it started or stopped. My work, as I recall, consisted of helping clean up the barn and, sometimes, helping spread cow manure on a field. Perhaps the strangest part of the job was my compensation: one egg per day. This type of compensation led to my involvement in retail transactions, for each day I sold the egg to my grandmother for a nickel.

Mention has been made of my work as a Western Union messenger during my mid-teen years. This entailed my spending a lot of time on my bike and thus improved my already considerable bike-riding skills. If I remember correctly, I could turn a corner while reading a comic book and without putting either of my hands on the handlebars. I fear this may be more wishful recollection. However, riding a bicycle with no hands on the handlebars was feasible only during good weather, and a Western Union messenger was on his bike in all kinds of weather. In the early darkness of many a winter day, I repeatedly became aware of the difficulties of piloting my bike along side streets covered with thick and rutted ice.

The largest employer in Elgin was the watch factory, and I worked there for a month when I was seventeen and during the summer when I turned twenty-two. Thousands of Elginites had worked at the watch factory for generations, and my dad was one of them. Many of these workers were laid off during the Depression, and my father was also one of them.

The summer when I worked at the watch factory was one of the summers when I had a job at the Elgin post office. The result was a very heavy schedule. During that summer I got up very early, walked about a half mile to the post office, threw incoming mail for folks who lived on one of the rural routes located in the countryside around Elgin, walked about a mile to the watch factory and put in an eight-hour day, then walked back to the post office and threw more incoming mail for the same rural route before finally walking back home.

My job at the watch factory during that summer was in the dial acid room and involved me with ruts of a different kind than the ruts in ice-covered winter streets. My main assignment was the electroplating of certain small parts for some kind of military equipment. This involved stringing these little items on racks that contained a series of hooks, submerging the racks and strips of cadmium metal in small tanks filled with some kind of cyanide solution, and then turning on the electricity running to the electrodes also submerged in the tanks.

A cyanide solution struck me as being something extremely dangerous, and I was surprised when the fellow who trained me on the cadmium plating job told me that some of the solution had once splashed into his mouth. My immediate reaction was to ask, "My gosh, what did you do?" His immediate response was, "I spit it out; what would you think I'd do?"

In order to get to my involvement with ruts, I'll have to give some further description of my electroplating procedures. Across an aisle from the plating tanks was another group of tanks, the rinsing tanks, which were the destination of the plated parts after the electricity had been on at the plating tanks for the specified time. I then removed the racks and shook them over the tanks with the objective of returning as much of the cyanide solution to the plating tanks as possible without dislodging any of the newly plated parts from their hooks. The next step was across the aisle, where I dipped the racks first in an acid-filled tank, next in a water-filled tank, then another acid and another water, shaking the racks after each dip into a rinsing tank and finally hanging up the racks so that the plated parts could dry.

Naturally, because I did these same operations over and over again during most of the summer, I made the same movements and took the same steps, across and along the aisle, over and over again. The way this worked out, the racks of newly plated parts (which always had remnants of the cyanide solution on them while they were en route across the aisle to the rinsing tanks) passed directly over my left shoe as I stepped across the aisle and dripped a little cyanide solution on my left shoe each time. I'm sure you have the picture now. By the end of the summer my right shoe looked like a shoe, and my left shoe looked…well, rutted.

The room where I did the electroplating richly deserved its name, the acid room, for there were cauldrons and other containers where various types of acids were busily bubbling away. We even had some hydrofluoric acid, which had to be kept in a lead container because it would eat through anything else. I was, of course, aware of one use made of acid in that room but had no idea what other purposes were served by the various acids.

Before I started my cadmium-plating work, I had other assignments in the acid room for a short time, one of which was annealing watch dials in an electric furnace at a temperature of 1,300 degrees Fahrenheit. One day an annealed piece happened to pop out of the basket and fall onto the floor as I was withdrawing the basket of annealed pieces from the furnace. I automatically reached down to pick up what had fallen. Try to imagine how sorry I was about that!

One summer during my college years, I worked in the inspection and shipping departments at a foundry. One day, when I was wheeling a cart through the shop, I felt a pinch on the back of my leg. I thought one of the guys was horsing around, but when I turned I saw a little dog scurrying away. I had been bitten by a dog which I hadn't even seen prior to the bite! I immediately checked and found that my skin had not been broken by the bite, so I didn't pursue the matter—or the dog.

A couple of days during that summer I spent shoveling something called silica dust. I don't know what that stuff is good for, but I know what it's bad for—lungs. I believe I spit black for a week after my brief connection with silica dust.

I also had jobs during a couple of summers and at college during a couple of school years that could be regarded as clerk-typist positions. I had learned to type by taking a course in high school from a teacher by the name of George Peck. He always claimed that he had nothing to do with the hunt-and-peck system. Years later, several of my children had typewriters and learned to type during their high school years. One of them was curious as to why I would take a typing course in school when it is so easy to learn by oneself at home, but she, of course, understood when I pointed out that in those earlier times a typewriter for me was not something my parents were in a position to buy.

During high school and college days, I also had busboy-type jobs, one of which was at the freshman dining hall at college. This called for a very early alarm clock setting on the days when I worked, often after I had had very little sleep. As a result, I was usually very sleepy during the first class or two after the completion of my shift at the dining hall. I recall one set of notes I made under these circumstances during an hour-long lecture relating to medieval European history. My notes read something like "lords—vassals—serfs—feudal system—chivalry." There's an hour's worth of learning for you.

Chapter 21

La(w) La(w) Land

Preamble

Know all men by these presents that, almost since the mind of man runneth not to the contrary, I was an attorney and counselor at law, as heretofore avowed, conceded, and acknowledged hereinabove; and, furthermore and moreover, this indenture witnesseth that I became said attorney in accordance, conformity, and compliance with all laws, statutes, ordinances, rules, regulations, and requirements in such case made and provided.

Wherein I Am En Route to, to wit, La(w) La(w) Land

In the days of my youth, I had no ambition to become a lawyer and, at the time I went away to college, had a vague objective of becoming some sort of a scientist. I had long been interested in science and, from time to time during my youthful years, had fooled around with a little chemistry set in the basement of our house. One day I managed to tip over my alcohol lamp while I was working (or playing) with my chemistry set. I then contemplated a pool of burning alcohol on my linoleum-covered work surface and also contemplated the question whether I should call to my mother upstairs, to tell her I had started a fire, or should try to put out the fire myself. Luckily, I almost immediately saw a way to do the latter—I threw an asbestos pad on the fire and the flames were quelled at once. In those days asbestos was good!

Several years later, in my first semester at college, any thoughts of a career in science were completely squelched when I took an accelerated chemistry course. I simply didn't understand this course at all and considered myself lucky just to get a passing grade. It's no doubt just as well that I didn't go into science, for I recall that my laboratory technique was not that of a scientist. When it came to measuring quantities of chemicals or other substances involved in a lab experiment, I took kind of a ballpark approach and usually concluded that the quantities I used in the experiment were "close enough" to the prescribed quantities.

After giving up any scientific ambitions, I drifted through several majors in college and, with an occasional nudge from my family, drifted toward law school. During my senior year in college, I took the Law School Aptitude Test, a prerequisite for admission to almost any law school. The LSAT consisted of a number of sections, with a specified time limit for completion of each section. During the test there was a break, for purposes of stretching legs, smoking, etc., just before a section for which the allotted time was eight minutes. I accordingly lit up my pipe, as this was during one of those time periods when I had given up cigarettes. When it was time to resume the test, I put my pipe in the pocket of my jacket, which was lying on the seat next to where I was sitting. Moments after I had resumed working on the test, I noticed that smoke was coming from my jacket, and then I spent more of the eight-minute time limit than I wanted to extinguishing pipe, jacket, and whatever else seemed to be smoldering.

Although my performance on that particular section of the LSAT was no doubt wanting, I did well enough overall to be admitted to the law schools to which I applied, including the law school at the university where I was attending college. I decided, however, to go to the University of Michigan instead.

The dormitory room to which I was assigned for my first year at Michigan happened to look right across the street to an undergraduate girls' dormitory, and my roommate happened to have a pair of binoculars. We soon developed a system of assigning names to various windows in the girls' dorm, so that if either of us saw anything of potential interest through a particular window, he could call out the window's name, and the other guy would immediately know just where to look. The binoculars got passed back and forth quite a bit. I know what we were looking for, but they weren't anything we hadn't seen before. And, as I believe Jack Benny once said, if you've seen two, you've seen them all.

Something that surprised me about law school was that, unlike college, students were assigned seats in each class and attendance was taken. In addition, law school involved much more classroom participation in the way of answering questions posed by the professors. However, the fact that you were called on in class didn't necessarily mean that you would recite, for it was usually possible to escape by uttering the magic word "Pass," though such nonparticipation could have some impact on your grade in the course. I made use of the magic word from time to time when I didn't know the answer to the question or hadn't listened to the question or was occupied in working on something other than the subject of that particular class. And I heard a story, probably apocryphal, that one of my classmates went so far as to say "Pass" when the professor asked him to close the door to the lecture hall.

In the early days of each semester, many students attended classes in a variety of courses before deciding exactly what ones they would take, and the assigning of seats was generally put off until things settled down and the class attendees included only those who had actually decided to take the particular course. As a result of the process, when it came time to assign seats there were always a lot of empty seats scattered around, where the course shoppers who didn't ultimately sign up had sat during the first days of the semester. The professors usually liked to move people around at this point in time so as to fill up the empty seats near the front of the hall, in order to make it easier to take attendance and generally keep track of things.

The preceding paragraph is the prologue to an anecdote I want to relate concerning seat assignments. The first chapter of the story occurred at the start of my junior year in law school, when I was in a class taught by Professor Palmer. One day when the professor was engaged in the customary process of persuading students to move from the back of the lecture hall to various empty seats in the front rows, one of these students resisted Palmer's blandishments, claiming that his seat near the back was just dandy and that he could hear the professor just fine. Palmer let him be, for a week or two, until the day when he observed that the student was sound asleep in his dandy seat near the back of the lecture hall. There were no negotiations this time, and the student was summarily summoned to a seat in the front row.

At the beginning of the second semester of my senior year, in another course taught by Professor Palmer, a similar scene unfolded in a different classroom. Again, that same student was comfortably ensconced in a seat near the back of the room; again, Palmer was seeking to move students from the back into the empty seats now available near the front; and again this student was resisting Palmer's efforts to coax him to move. After this went on for a little while, the professor suddenly cocked his head, looked at the student, and said, "Haven't you and I gone through this before?"

One of the things I had learned along the way in college (and which I found to be equally true in law school) was that the extent of my preparation for a final exam seemed to have little to do with my performance on the exam and, hence, my grade in the course. Perhaps this is why there was at least one time in college when I let Don, my high school and college classmate, talk me into going out to drink beer for a few hours the night before I did (and he did not) have a final examination scheduled. Also, there is such a thing as becoming overprepared for an exam. I heard that one guy I knew in law school stayed up all night getting ready for an exam and then went in to take the exam and fell asleep.

Final examinations in most college and law school courses that I took were almost exclusively of the essay type, calling for lengthy and well-thought-out answers. Like most students, I generally found myself writing fast and furiously throughout the exam period and trying to think as fast as I was writing. Therefore, I was pretty surprised at one law school exam when I found out that I had finished several minutes before the expiration of the three-hour time period. For some reason I then idly leafed through the exam booklet and—horrors—found that I had not turned a page that I should have turned long since. Now that I turned that page, I found that it was followed by some fifty multiple choice and true-or-false questions and that I had five minutes to deal with them. Here was a case where my answers would be neither lengthy nor, I fear, well thought out.

In due course, I got through law school and landed a job with a Chicago law firm, but only after becoming a married man following my freshman year and becoming the father of Laura during my senior year.

Wherein I Am Domiciled in, to wit, La(w) La(w) Land

The law firm where I started to work upon graduation from law school shall be known here as Martin, Barton & Fargo. That is, of course, a joke name (and by no means original with me), but my mother-in-law, Lucille, didn't get the joke. I forget now whether I told her that was the name of my employer because I just wanted to make a joke or because I had told her the actual name several times and she kept forgetting it. Lucille's failure to get the joke is no sign of stupidity on her part, for she was quite an intelligent woman. It's just that she was on a different wavelength—she wasn't into scatology at all. In any case, it is my understanding that Lucille told some of her friends that her son-in-law Paul worked for a Chicago law firm named Martin, Barton & Fargo. I can only hope that her friends didn't get the joke either.

One of my first assignments at the Martin firm was to monitor the responses of the firm's principal client to garnishment proceedings filed anywhere in the country. Briefly, garnishment was a method used by creditors of the client's employees to collect portions of the wages payable to those employees and to apply the amounts collected to judgments that the creditors had obtained against the employees. My task was to make sure that the client filed timely answers in garnishment proceedings stating the amounts of wages owed to the employees involved.

Perhaps a month or two after I started working for the Martin firm, it came to my attention that a creditor of an employee at the client's Atlanta office or plant was seeking to garnish the employee's wages as a means of collecting the $29 unpaid balance of a judgment. As I recall, I became aware of this the day before the answer in the garnishment proceeding was due to be filed. The sum of $29 meant more in those days than it does now, of course, but it didn't mean much in those days either. Still, my assignment was to make sure that our client filed timely answers in all garnishment proceedings. I discussed the matter with the attorney who had handled such garnishments before my arrival at the firm and, pursuant to that discussion, called the Atlanta office to make sure that the client was ready to file its answers in the proceeding on the following day.

The call was made to the appropriate person in Atlanta, and he assured me that everything was under control and that the proper filing would be made. He went on to say that Mr. Loomis wanted to talk to me, and another voice then came on the phone and proceeded to chew me out and up and down and around the block for wasting time and money by calling long distance about a $29 garnishment. This gentleman further stated that the Atlanta office would take care of garnishments down there and that I should tend to my own knitting. My response, if any, was neither memorable nor remembered.

At the time this episode occurred, the president of the client was a man I'll call Claude Loomis, and when I discussed the incident at lunch with a couple of colleagues a day or two later, I speculated as to whether the president of our client had lambasted me over the telephone as I have described. My colleagues were certain that I must have talked to someone else named Loomis and ridiculed me for even suggesting the possibility that Claude Loomis would waste his time talking to me, especially about such an insignificant matter. So I thought no further about the incident—for a week or two.

About that long after the events I have described, Mr. Martin came into my office and mentioned that he and Barton had recently had a conversation with Claude Loomis, in the course of which Loomis complained about a long distance call from our office to Atlanta concerning a $29 garnishment. Mr. Martin figured that I was probably the caller and, upon my acknowledging the accuracy of his supposition, suggested that I use better judgment in the future than to spend time on a $29 garnishment. My reaction—unexpressed, of course—was that I was the junior member of an otherwise illustrious group of personages that had devoted time to a $29 garnishment.

Thereafter, I believe I got back in Mr. Martin's good graces. As I was walking from the train station to the office one morning, a hat propelled by the wind came bouncing and rolling past me. I chased after it, picked it up, and turned around to find that the owner of the hat (out of the scores of people walking along that sidewalk) was none other than Mr. Martin.

However, soon after I joined Martin, Barton & Fargo, it became apparent to me, as it was to everyone else, that Barton was the main man and that the place to be was on his good side. And, wouldn't you know it, I was assigned to areas of the firm's practice in which Mr. Barton was not at all involved. My work was principally in the area of property law, and I am reminded of a brief conversation I had with Mr. Barton at the time I interviewed with the firm before being hired. Barton inquired as to what subjects I had particularly enjoyed in law school, and I said something to the effect that I had found the future interests course (which dealt with an area of property law) challenging and interesting. Barton responded (in a somewhat boastful manner, I thought) that he wouldn't know a future interest if he ran into one on the street. I recognize that ignorance is nothing to be ashamed of but also think that it's nothing to brag about.

Mr. Barton and I lived in two different worlds, and (even though there were only twenty or thirty lawyers in the firm) this was pretty much true of all the senior partners and all the young associates, except in cases where a particular associate worked for a particular partner on a regular basis. This is borne out by an incident in which I was not involved but which I heard about later on. A lawyer who started with the Martin firm upon his graduation from law school and moved on to another firm after a couple of years dropped in to the firm's office one day about six months after his move and was chatting in our law library with a couple of his former colleagues. One of the senior partners walked into the library looking for an associate to undertake a legal research project. He saw and recognized this fellow and requested that he take on the assignment, evidently having no idea that he had long since left the firm. He went along with the senior partner and said that he would get right on the project.

At any rate, after I had been with the firm for a couple of years, I finally received a summons to report to Mr. Barton's office because he had an assignment for me. Try to imagine the excitement and anticipation I felt at the prospect of at last working directly for the big guy. Well, Mr. Barton had an assignment for me, all right. He directed me to help carry the luggage of a visiting client over to the railroad station.

Actually, a good while later I did get an assignment from Barton that involved legal work and a trip to a number of cities in southern Illinois. A young lawyer from New York City was to work with me on this project, and we were to meet at the St. Louis airport and drive a rented car from there. This trip began in late November, and unfortunately quite a blizzard was under way when the New Yorker and I met in St. Louis. We set out in our car anyway, with me as the driver, inasmuch as I was more familiar with the territory. As you would expect when a snowstorm is going on, there were dreadful traffic problems. We must have spent close to half an hour on one of the bridges over the Mississippi River, and when we got to the Illinois side, we again found ourselves sitting in a long line of traffic. Finally I decided that we should go back to St. Louis and then try another bridge in hopes that there would be less of a tie-up. Accordingly, I made a U-turn and headed back over the bridge. As we recrossed the bridge, I said to my companion, "Well, here we are out of Illinois and back in Missouri," and his comment was, "Say, what's the boundary, anyway?" He must have been one of those provincial New Yorkers who think that civilization extends no farther west than the Connecticut River.

In my young lawyer days I wore a suit every day. On one occasion I might have given our receptionist the impression that I was trying to start a new style in men's fashions, for she pointed out to me that the back of my suit jacket was tucked into my trousers. Thereafter, when I installed myself in the throne room, I took off my jacket before getting down to business.

As long as we're back to scatology, I'll relate one other incident that occurred some years later. First, though, I want to mention that I've noticed, and perhaps you have too, that in an office or other work environment where a reasonably small number of people are using the same bathroom facilities (a men's room, in my experience), you are often able to identify the colleague who is located in a particular stall, just from the sound of his coughs, grunts, sighs, snorts, sniffs, ahems, and harrumphs. (I won't mention any other types of sounds.)

On the occasion I'll describe here, I was enthroned in one of the four stalls in the Martin, Barton & Fargo men's room, and I became aware that the managing partner of the firm was situated in the stall at the far end of the row of four. I was also aware that (1) the toilet in the stall where he was situated had recently seemed to be clogged, and (2) repeated flushing of a clogged toilet would likely cause an unpleasant overflow. When I heard him finishing up, I decided that perhaps I should also make ready to depart…just in case. He flushed once, and I thought, "Don't do it again." He flushed twice, and I thought, "You idiot, you did it again." He flushed thrice, said, "Uh-oh, it's coming your way," and left. And, as I made my own escape, I thought, "That is not the kind of leadership this firm needs." Now, I'm not trying to say that our managing partner was a four-flusher, but he was close.

From time to time I had various types of problems with secretaries, and I'll favor you with a couple memorable stories. On one occasion I asked my secretary to finalize a letter, the draft of which included the following: ["Chicago address"]. The address in question was readily available in the file, and I assumed that my secretary would insert it. She apparently preferred to handle the matter in a different way, for the finalized letter included the following: ["Chicago address"].

I had a different problem with a different secretary, to whom I had given a draft of a document to type. Upon my later inquiring with her concerning the completed document, she denied receiving the draft. When the draft was later found in her waste basket, she accused me of planting it there!!

At some point in my career at the Martin firm, I became aware of the desirability of developing expertise in particular areas of the law and becoming a specialist. I also recognized that I had had experience in a couple of situations where it would be very unlikely that I would have to compete with many other specialists. One of these was the negotiation and preparation of a lease of space in a cave for use as a cold storage facility, and the other was handling the estates of spouses whose deaths resulted from a murder and a suicide. Unfortunately, in all the years thereafter, I never had the opportunity to handle any other cave lease or murder-suicide estates, and I remained pretty much a generalist.

Two of my good friends at the Martin firm were Chub Dawson and Dan Hasenpfeffer (their real names are just as strange). The three of us and some of our other partners often had lunch together. Sometimes Chub would tell the rest of us that he had to make a stop at the old hangout before going to lunch and that he would be with us in two shakes of a lamb's tail. I always assumed that Chub was speaking metaphorically and that he was not some sort of mutant.

Dan was considered kind of a messy eater, and on some occasions, perhaps while waiting for the lunch group to assemble or while riding down in the elevator, Chub would take hold of Dan's tie, inspect it, and then offer an opinion as to what Dan had had for breakfast.

There was, of course, a lot of conversation at the lunch table, and more often than not the subject was shop talk and office politics. On one occasion Dan mentioned that, at the last minute, he had been roped into attending a meeting, relating to some case with which he was not familiar, but that it was okay because all he had to do was sit there and look intelligent. Though my memory's not clear about this, I may have asked him how he managed to look intelligent and whether he had worn a mask.

Generally, at the restaurants where we had lunch a single check was provided for the entire group. Instead of dividing the bill equally among those in attendance, we traditionally followed a more complicated system. Hasenpfeffer served as cashier and endeavored to determine exactly how much of the check was attributable to each of us. This procedure involved various questions, such as "Who had the iced tea?" and various comments, such as, "Your tip should be sixty-five cents, not fifty cents." It usually took quite some time for Dan to complete his determinations. The rest of us suspected that Dan somehow made a profit out of his cashier function, but we were never able to prove anything. Because an attorney's time is regarded (by attorneys at least) as quite valuable, we tried to spend no more than fifteen minutes per day in determining just how our lunch checks should be divvied up.

During a few years at the Martin firm, I worked closely with a young lawyer by the name of Ed, and we became good friends. He was an excellent chess player, and I told him that I had played chess when I was young, though I had learned that I was very far from being a whiz. Ed from time to time had played chess while blindfolded and suggested that we have a match, to see whether he could beat me while playing blindfolded. I considered this but then decided not to play him when I found out that he would expect me to tell him, on each move, which chess piece I had moved and where I had moved it. I complained to Ed that he had agreed to play blindfolded and was now trying to renege on the deal. Sheesh!

A number of years ago, Martin, Barton & Fargo and I parted company and I joined another Chicago law firm. Shortly after that a long-time client and friend of mine died unexpectedly, leaving a will naming me as her executor. The will left a substantial part of her estate in trust for a distant relative, who was a minor living with his mother, and also named me as the trustee to administer that trust. As I recall, I considered it inappropriate for me to contact the trust beneficiary or his mother until the will had been admitted to probate and I had been appointed as executor. Due to various red tape, this did not occur until about six weeks after the death of my friend. In the meantime, the mother of the trust beneficiary evidently heard through the grapevine that some money had been left to her son by a distant relative who had recently died. As I learned later, she hired a Chicago law firm to investigate the situation and obtain detailed information as to her son's inheritance, and the partner whom she contacted at that law firm asked one of the young lawyers in the firm to handle the project.

During this time period—that is, after my friend's death and before my appointment as executor—I stopped at a local watering hole after work one evening to have a beer with a young lawyer in our firm whose office happened to be right next to mine. We talked about a variety of things, and in the course of our conversation, it came out that I was handling my friend's estate and trust, that our law firm was the very firm that had been contacted by the trust beneficiary's mother, and that the fellow I was sharing a couple of beers with was the young lawyer who had been assigned to the project and who had been seeking to gather information regarding the trust beneficiary's inheritance. Proof, once again, that the world can indeed be small.

Because my personal clients were few and far between, I did not have a lot of portable business to bring with me to this other law firm and did not become a partner in the firm. However, it was apparently considered somewhat awkward to refer to a lawyer as, shall we say, experienced as I by the designation of associate. Accordingly, not long after I joined this firm, I was designated as a member of the firm. I recall that on a few later occasions, one or another partner in the firm introduced me to an outsider as that partner's associate. I was inclined to be a little miffed about this but, upon further consideration, decided that I did not expect or want a partner to introduce me as his member.

Although I eventually had a computer on my desk, virtually all of the other lawyers in the office had computers for years before I did, either because I had an of-counsel status, rather than an employee status, with the firm or because the powers that be had heard that I didn't do Windows.

Not long after I joined this law firm, I got in the habit of shooting the breeze from time to time with Stu, one of the younger lawyers in the firm. I don't know how this got started, except that it definitely was at his initiative. Ever since, I have much appreciated the fact that Stu took the first step or two in establishing a friendship with an old fart like me, with no clout in the firm. In one of our conversations, Stu told me of a disagreement he had had at his health club with another club member concerning the use of some exercise apparatus. The upshot was that the other club member called Stu a bald-headed asshole and then stalked off. Now, Stu is indeed pretty much bald, but I have assured him again and again that I would not consider him a bald-headed asshole—a nonhirsute cloaca, perhaps, but surely not a bald-headed asshole.

During my early years with the firm, almost all of the other lawyers there were Jewish. One day when I was in the office of one of my Jewish colleagues, talking with him about something or other, we noticed a hornet flying around. He tried to shoo the hornet away, saying as he did so, "Get out of here. We don't allow any wasps in here." And then, turning to me, continued: "Except, of course, for you, Paul."

Postscript

As you may recall, I began this chapter with a preamble setting forth an example of what is commonly disparaged as legalese. My purpose now is to set forth a theory (obviously not original with me) as to one reason why lawyers use legalese.

Much of the law concerning the meaning the words, phrases, sentences, and paragraphs that appear in documents of various sorts comes from decisions rendered by courts of appeal over the years. Accordingly, when a court decides that a particular clause or provision in a contract, a will, a lease, or another document means such and such, attorneys who subsequently prepare a similar document and want their document also to mean such and such tend to use the same language that has already received an appellate court's stamp of approval. Attorneys know that if a single word is changed, this may open a door to a court putting a different and unwanted interpretation upon the document now being prepared by the attorney.

Many contract, will, lease, and other documentary clauses and provisions that were construed and approved in court decisions years ago therefore found their way into forms for such documents. Once a clause or provision is in a form, it obviously stands a better chance of being incorporated into countless documents of that type and, also, in subsequent forms developed for such documents.

Certainly inertia and lethargy are also among the factors that contribute to the perpetuation of legalese. Acting along with such factors, it seems to me, is a tendency to use language that was interpreted and approved by an appellate court in the past and that has apparently worked ever since.

Chapter 22

Telephone Troubles

We have all had and no doubt will continue to have telephone troubles. Some are the fault of the telephone company—for example, being billed for calls (to information or elsewhere) that were never made or dialing a number and finding ourselves listening in (at least briefly) to a conversation between two other people who cannot hear us. Other troubles—including interminable and/or confusing menus and the practice of requiring callers who remain on hold to listen to dreadful music or, worse, dreadful commercials—are the fault of such phone company customers as banks, stores, corporations, etc. There are also troubles that happen because of the way the world is and that are really nobody's fault. One instance of this happened to me when I stayed on hold for several minutes while waiting for a client to finish some other telephone conversation so that I could speak to him about something rather urgent. This went on until my secretary came into my office with a note that the client needed to talk to me and had been holding for several minutes.

My most frequent telephone trouble is the failure of the telephone company or its employees to understand how my last name is pronounced. The letter "a" in Gabler is pronounced just as that letter is pronounced in the following instruction from yesteryear, when things were much less expensive than they are nowadays—namely, "Get off the table, Mabel, the twenty-five cents is for the beer."

There have been a multitude of instances where I have explained to a phone company employee how to pronounce Gabler and where later in the same conversation with the same employee the name is pronounced repeatedly with the "a" being pronounced as it is in the word "as." There have also been occasions when the telephone company employee pronounces my last name as "Gobbler."

If I am able to convince my auditor to say my name with "a" properly pronounced, that doesn't necessarily end my troubles, for then my last name is often pronounced by phone company employees as "Gabriel" or, in one case, "Gaybar." Years ago we were unable to convince our service provider to spell or say our last name in any way other than "Gabriel," either orally or in writing.

Late in my tenure at Martin, Barton & Fargo, the modern telephone system arrived. One of the features of our system was the group pickup, whereby I could answer a telephone ringing in a nearby office if that phone wasn't picked up within a specified number of rings. One day, shortly after 5 p.m., I was sitting in my office talking to a colleague, Susan, who had an office near mine. We heard a phone ringing and, though I didn't know whose phone it was, I knew it was in our neighborhood and therefore pushed the appropriate button and picked up. I heard a voice on the phone whisper these words: "You will die at ten o'clock."

What should I have done in a crisis such as this: (1) hang up the phone? or (2) hand the phone to Susan and say, "It's for you"? I hung up the phone and never learned the identity of the caller.

Many years earlier, I had some telephone trouble of a different sort: a call one night that came in while I was sound asleep, at about 4 a.m. Upon awakening and picking up the phone in the bedroom, I heard the caller inquire as to whether he had reached the Sportsman's Park racetrack hotline. When I responded that he had indeed reached the hotline, his next inquiry was as to the winner of the seventh race. After answering "Beedlebaum" in a loud voice, I slammed down the phone.

For those of you not familiar with Beedlebaum, that was a horse involved in a well-known, at one time anyway, comedy record made by Doodles Weaver with the Spike Jones Band. In that record Doodles reports on a horse race in detail, listing the horses in order at each of four or five stages of the race, and concluding in each case with the words "And in last place, Beedlebaum." But finally, Doodles ends his description of the race with some such statement as "At the finish line, the winner is Beedlebaum!"

For those of you not familiar with Doodles or Spike, ask your parents… or grandparents.

Long after that late-night call, Nancy received a phone call from some unknown male caller and felt much harassed by what he had to say. At about the same time, I was at the office and wanted to talk to Nancy in order to make sure that she was remembering to record some TV show we wanted to watch that night. When I called our home phone for that purpose, Nancy feared it was the caller who had harassed her and immediately hung up the phone.

After the foregoing scenario had been repeated several times, a solution occurred to me and I sent Nancy the following fax: "Please answer the phone." After she had a good laugh, she called me; we talked; everything worked out all right.

Our most recent telephone trouble arose when we moved from Illinois to Indiana and acquired a different area code and phone number. For weeks thereafter, some of the persons we telephoned reported to us that a name different than ours appeared on their telephone screen as the caller. It took us many weeks and many calls to our provider to get this matter resolved, for the former holder of our new number was deceased and some input was also needed from his telephone service provider.

When it comes to telephone menus, my practice (in order to do whatever I can to reduce the time spent listening to the damn things) is to press the appropriate key immediately when I become aware of what key will give me the selection I want, and to enter numbers and other data as soon as requested. I employed this practice one Sunday afternoon when I telephoned the automated prescription refill service (which I'll call Acme Prescription Service) used by our group health insurer. The following is the verbatim result:

Thank you for calling [Acme Prescription Service]. If you would like to place a refill order or check the status of an order through [Acme Prescription Service's] automated prescription line, please press 1 now. You have selected [Acme Prescription Service's] automated services line. If you should make an error at any time, press the star key. Please listen to the following menu options. To order a refill, press 2. You have selected [Acme Prescription Service's] automated refill line.

Please enter your plan identification number as it appears in the upper left-hand corner of your refill reorder form. Follow it by the pound sign. You have entered identification number [specified number]. If this is correct, press 2.

Please enter your prescription refill number, followed by the pound sign. You have entered prescription refill number [specified number]. If this is correct, press 2. To order another refill, press 2. If you have no additional refills, press 3.

Please enter your complete credit card number, followed by the pound sign. Please enter the card's expiration month, followed by the pound sign. Please enter the card's expiration year, followed by the pound sign. Please wait while your request is being processed. [This sentence was repeated seven times, with a dead air pause before each repeat.]

We are sorry we are unable to process your request at this time. [Acme Prescription Service] is now closed. [Acme Prescription Service's] hours of operation are 7 a.m. to 8 p.m., Monday through Friday, and 8 a.m. to 2 p.m., Saturday, Central Standard Time. We are closed Sundays and holidays. Please call back during normal business hours so that an [Acme Prescription Service] representative may assist you.

Chapter 23

In Memory of Beloved Manny

Although Manny has been dead for many years now, Nancy still thinks of him every day. And this is by no means a case of someone mourning for the only pet cat she ever had. At the time Manny came into Nancy's life, she and her mother, who lived together at the time, had a number of other cats: Alfie, Becky, Bozo, Buffy, Rocky, Shamus, and Tiggy. But Manny was a special cat, and memories of Manny are special—to me as well as to Nancy.

Shortly after Manny's death, the city did some renovation work at a small park in the Chicago neighborhood where Nancy and I lived for many years. This work included the installation of a small brick plaza at the main entrance to the park. In return for a monetary contribution, the city would include in the plaza a brick bearing an inscription designated by the contributor. Nancy made such a contribution, and the inscription she selected is the title of this chapter.

When Manny first made his appearance, Nancy and her mother and all those other cats were living in a second-floor apartment on Lincoln Avenue, a major diagonal street on the north side of Chicago. They lived near one of those triple intersections resulting from the various diagonal streets in Chicago, but it was not the intersection of Lincoln, Blinkin, and Nodd.

In any event, Manny was then a neighborhood stray, and at some point Nancy spotted him, admired his appearance, and started leaving food out for him on the back porch. Then one thing led to another. Manny started eating the food put out for him, Nancy went out on the porch while

Manny was eating, Manny allowed Nancy to pet him and, later, to pick him up, and Nancy brought Manny inside the apartment for visits with the other cats. At an early stage in these proceedings, Nancy determined that Manny would be a better name for this stray cat than the name she had originally used, Mandy.

Later on I came into the picture and witnessed one of Manny's visits to the indoor cats. The cacophony of hisses and growls that went on throughout the visit was absolutely cacophonous. Even when Manny was out on the porch, sitting on an outside window sill, some of the indoor cats would hiss and growl and, also, claw at the window glass.

Although Nancy's other cats had made it clear that Manny would not be welcome, Nancy and I decided that, when we established our household, Manny would be a part of it. And this is what happened, for Manny went along with the plan even though I warned him that Nancy would have his balls cut off.

Manny never did get along with the other cats, except that he and Becky learned to play together. As a matter of fact, Manny may be the only cat Becky ever played with. Their favorite game seemed to be taking turns chasing one another around our three-level apartment. We would often look up to see Becky racing upstairs with Manny in hot pursuit, and moments later we would see Manny barreling back down the stairs with Becky right on his tail. Or vice versa.

Except for Becky, the other cats originally in our household were males (or had previously been males). Manny did not play with these other cats, but he did continually pick fights with some of them, and particularly with Tiggy. It seemed strange to us humans that Manny continued to be aggressive toward and start fights with Tiggy, for Manny was on the losing end of the fight at least 99 and 44/100 percent of the time.

Tiggy just wanted to be left alone. One of his favorite places to be alone was on top of a bookcase that stood next to the stairs leading to the second floor and was easily reached (if you were a cat) by squeezing through the metal grillwork that ran along the side of the staircase. I couldn't begin to count how many times Manny went up on those stairs and tried to bat at Tiggy when he was lying on top of that bookcase. Again Manny's conduct seemed strange to us humans, for what he was actually doing on these occasions was banging his paw, again and again, on that metal grillwork.

Of course, once Tiggy was aroused by Manny's attempted onslaught, he would try to strike back at Manny from the other side of the grillwork. So we could watch those two damn fools striking at each other and could listen to their paws hitting the iron grillwork, over and over again. Maybe cats don't have many pain cells in their paws.

Manny also caused problems for the humans in the household. Of all the cats either Nancy or I have ever owned, he was the only one who attempted to get into the fireplace and climb up the chimney. He was very determined about this, and, though he never got up the chimney, he was able to get into the fireplace about five times. Each time this happened, Manny was converted, temporarily, from a black and white cat into something quite close to an all-black cat. And each time Manny got into the fireplace, he followed it up with a soapy session in the stationary tub, and I followed it up with a session of trying again to secure our fireplace screen against Manny's possible future inroads. I don't recall exactly what I did but remember that it ultimately involved, among other things, drilling holes in bricks. In any event, I finally succeeded in my endeavor to prevent Manny from continuing to succeed in his endeavor.

Manny got into another place that we didn't want him to get into: a cabinet below a built-in counter in the lower level of the apartment. He was able to use his claws to pull the cabinet door open and then walked around inside the cabinet amongst bottles and other assorted crockery. Why he did this I don't know—probably just because it was there. When, in the course of one of these unlawful entries, Manny tipped over and spilled a bottle of liquor in the cabinet, I knew we had to take action to stop his depredations. We got one of those plastic hook-and-gizmo assemblies that are used to prevent small children from opening cabinet doors and found that they could also make a cabinet door Manny-proof.

Because Manny didn't like the other cats, he usually didn't congregate with them around the food dishes at mealtime. His practice was to eat when the others had finished. I once accidentally stepped on his tail when he was by the food dishes. By no means is this the only time I have ever stepped on a cat's tail, but Manny's reaction was unique. Generally a cat will screech and run away when you step on its tail. Manny, however, made no sound that I recall and grasped one of my legs in a not-so-fond embrace, until I shook him off. During the embrace, all four sets of Manny's claws were out (of their sheaths) and in (my leg).

In addition to being hostile to other cats—and to any human who stepped on his tail—Manny was mobile and agile. He demonstrated this one day when I was trying to catch him for some reason, perhaps to give him a good scolding concerning his fireplace or cabinet activities. I thought I had him cornered in the bedroom, but he suddenly leaped up and actually ran along the bedroom wall for several jumps and then out of the room and away.

Manny was not the world's smartest cat, as he demonstrated by his continued efforts to fight with Tiggy, despite losing every fight. He gave another such demonstration when he was outdoors on the upstairs deck with us one summer day. A tree in the courtyard of the apartment complex was close enough to the deck for squirrels to jump back and forth between the branches of the tree and the wall and railing around our deck, and Manny spotted a squirrel who had jumped over onto the wall. Manny crouched under a flower box that hung from the railing and, though he couldn't see the squirrel from where he was crouching, prepared to spring at the squirrel when he (the squirrel) came within reach. Naturally, as soon as he saw Manny, the squirrel jumped back to the tree. Manny, however, continued for some time to crouch under the hanging flower box, poised to spring. Finally, Nancy advised Manny as follows: "He's gone, Manny."

If Manny was hostile, mobile, agile, and dumb, why was he so beloved? The short answer is that there's no accounting for love, but I'll give you the long answer too, by describing—as best I can at this late date—what an affectionate, responsive, interesting, wonderful pet Manny was. From the outset, a point in Manny's favor, for me, was that he was the first joint Nancy-Paul pet. However, he had not been in our household very long before it started becoming apparent to me that Nancy also much preferred him over her other cats.

Most anyone who has been around cats knows what layabouts they are, and Manny had several places where he liked to do much of his lying about. These included that part of the sofa which happened to be the current location of a particular little white pillow that he liked to rest his head on, the top of the armchair back if Nancy or I happened to be sitting in the armchair, and the arm of the sofa adjacent to where Nancy or I happened to be sitting. Often when Manny was lying down, he pushed his face so hard into the sofa arm or his pillow that he almost seemed to be lying on his face. His position on the arm of the sofa frequently included a raised rump, which was his way of encouraging Nancy or me to pat him on the lower end of his back, right in front of his tail. While this patting was going on, Manny would often wrap his tail around the wrist of the person doing the patting. And if there was any interruption in the patting, Manny would usually turn his head and give Nancy or me a reproachful look.

When Nancy was in bed, Manny also liked to lie on her chest, with one front leg on each side of her neck and his face against hers. Nancy liked this too and treasures the memory of these times with her bestest kitty. However, except for this routine he and Nancy had, Manny did not like to lie on either of us or be held by either of us. He liked to be near us or beside us but was definitely not a lap cat. For example, if Nancy held Manny against her when she was standing up, he always seemed dissatisfied as to the position of one or another of his front legs, on her shoulder or around her neck, and made some adjustment. Although he was a gentleman about it and didn't squirm strenuously, Manny made it clear that he would prefer to be put back down on the floor. Like most cats, Manny felt more vulnerable near a person who was standing than near one who was lying down.

When I picked up Manny, my experience was similar to Nancy's, though I usually cradled him in my arms instead of holding him against me. Generally he would look up at me and gently strain or push off a little to let me know that he would like to be set down. If I held on to him instead of setting him down, he would look away and then, moments later, look back at me and repeat the procedure.

This procedure of Manny's when I was holding him was one situation where I think Manny displayed what a graceful cat he was. This quality was also demonstrated by the manner in which Manny turned away—for example, when he was walking toward me and I reached for him as if to pick him up. He didn't just turn tail and skedaddle but, instead, just veered to the side and slowly turned away with kind of a little toss of his head. For years Nancy and I referred to graceful movements like these as "Manny moves." A Manny move is one of those things that is very difficult to describe, but I do know one when I see one.

Although Manny didn't like to be picked up or held, he of course liked to be petted. He found a way to achieve both of his objectives on those innumerable occasions when he was hanging around or passing by while I sat at our table doing legal or household paperwork. He liked to stand under the chair on which I was sitting, and it almost seemed that, in doing so, he was intentionally putting himself in a position where I could reach down to pet him but not to pick him up.

Manny was a cat who liked face-petting. When he was being petted while standing, he would often rise up on his hind legs and thrust his face upward into the human hand that was petting him. Manny also learned to rise up in this manner in response to Nancy's snapping of her fingers.

He was not a particularly vocal cat. His purr was extremely light. There were occasions when he would quietly mew at Nancy or me, the most frequent instance being when she was in the shower and Manny was sitting on the floor next to the shower, apparently imploring her to hurry up and come out to where he could be with her again. Although I took showers also, I don't recall that Manny ever mewed at me to encourage me to hurry up and finish. However, in mild weather when the windows were open, I would often find Manny mewing at me through the window screen when I came back from taking the garbage out to the trash barrel.

Not all of Nancy's original cats were in the household during the few years that Manny was with us. A couple of the other cats stayed with Nancy's mother, and another died before Manny. About three years after Manny came into the household, we got a new arrival, a little female kitten we named Ginger, who had been born in a barn out in the far suburbs at the place where a friend of Nancy stabled her horse.

When Ginger was a kitten, she was a holy terror to the older cats, jumping at them, biting their tails, and otherwise annoying and tormenting them. All of the older cats naturally tried to avoid Ginger and have nothing to do with her—all except Manny. Manny played with her. They spent a lot of time romping around together, and in one of their games they would run at one another and each leap into the air as they met. In all of their games, Manny was quite gentle with Ginger, far more gentle than she was with him.

Manny played with his mommy and daddy too, and I especially remember our game involving a thin plastic band and the open staircase leading up to the second floor. That staircase was right above the stairs leading down into the lower level, and the game consisted of (1) Nancy or me standing on the lower staircase and thrusting the plastic band between two of the upper stairs and (2) Manny standing on the upper staircase and trying to seize the plastic band before we pulled it back out of his reach. We played the game so often that it got to the point where I could pick up a plastic band, head for the lower staircase, say, "You wanna play?" to Manny, and he would dash for the upper staircase and peer through one of the between-stairs openings.

Sometimes during the plastic band game, Manny was quick enough to grab the band, and sometimes we let him grab it. Each time he got hold of the band, we of course pulled it free of his claws and/or teeth and then repeated the process, sometimes shifting to an opening between different stairs. As the process of tempting, seizing (or trying to seize), and pulling back was repeated over and over again, Manny's eyes would look more and more feral. But no matter how excited he got and how quickly he grabbed at the plastic band when it was thrust between the stairs, whenever I put my hand (rather than the band) through the opening, Manny never clawed it or touched it. Instead, he would immediately stop and look at me as if to say, "Quit fooling around and get back to the game."

About a year after Ginger's arrival, Manny became ill, gradually got worse during the course of a couple of months, and then died. We believed he was not suffering pain during this time, and we therefore did not have him put to sleep, as we have done with a number of other cats over the years. He gradually faded away and remained in the apartment with us to the end. He was a very special pet, and we arranged to have him buried—and to have his little white pillow buried with him.

My memory of Manny's illness is hazy, but I think there were few, if any, specific symptoms and he just exhibited a general, and increasing, malaise. The veterinarian finally decided that Manny was afflicted with a parasite that was somehow destroying his red blood cells, but I don't recall that I ever knew the name of the disease or condition. We tried to save him and even had him given a very large transfusion of blood.

He remained responsive to the end. As he lay dying and as we petted him and told him what a good boy he was, he mewed very softly to us.

Nancy was upstairs with him when he died. When she called me to tell me he was gone, I ran upstairs to find her standing there sobbing and holding his dead body clutched against her. As I watched them through my own tears, I saw that, at last, Manny was not straining quietly to show his desire to be set down and was not making any effort to adjust the position of his front legs on her shoulder.

Chapter 24

More Cats and a Few Other Pets

Preamble

Over the years, various pets have come into and gone out of my life. One of them, Manny, was of course the subject of the preceding chapter. As to the others, I will say something about some of them in the following pages.

Heinz

He was the dog of my children's childhood and was definitely a mixed breed. Hence, Heinz. Although he was a nice dog, Heinz had problems and created problems for us. I fear that most of the problems stemmed from our failure to have certain surgery performed on him. Maybe he was too old for the surgery when we got him, or maybe I just don't remember.

In any case, Heinz liked to get out and roam the neighborhood. Sometimes when our daughters were leaving for school, Heinz would see a chance to escape, burst through the doorway, and send little girls flying, tea over asskettle, in all directions. (Here again, I pay no attention to the fact that my mother had told me, sixty million times, not to exaggerate.)

One day a neighbor came to our house, dog in tow, and said that he had spotted Heinz down the block and had brought him back. As it happened, Heinz was already in the house. The other dog was pretty near a dead ringer for Heinz and was probably one of his descendants.

Ed and Tom arrived during Heinz's sojourn in our family, and Heinz and Ed shared in one activity during Ed's first year when he was in the creepy-crawly stage. Sometimes when Heinz was lying on the floor gnawing on a bone, Ed would creep over to join the dog and attempt to put the other end of the bone in his own mouth. Because Ed was the fourth child, his parents were well aware by then that babies are not noted for cleanliness and try to put in their mouths whatever they can get hold of.

Heinz was quite trainable in some ways; for example, he would go down to the basement and lie in his bed when I told him to go to bed. I worked on training him to heel, and sometimes he would heel even when he was not on a leash. He would obey the command to sit, which of course is elementary. But what I think was unusual is that if I told him to sit at a time when he happened to be lying down, he would get up and then sit without any further command.

When Heinz was out in the backyard, he was on a line attached to a stake driven into the ground. Accordingly, periodic patrols of the Heinz area were called for and were, for example, a prerequisite to any lawn-mowing or leaf-raking activities. Such patrols were made somewhat easier by the facts that (1) with five little kids in the family, there were lots of crayons around the house, and (2) Heinz liked to eat crayons. Heinz's digestive system did not share his liking for crayons, so the crayon pieces passed right on through intact and made certain things easier to spot.

The Cats of My First Incarnation

Not long after the death of Heinz, Barbara's parents gave us a little white kitten that we named Sugar. She was a good and happy pet for a time. One of the interesting things she did had to do with the fact that, when cars were driven down the street past our house at night, their headlights caused light to flash along the walls in certain parts of the house. Sugar located one such area, on the wall next to the staircase leading to the second floor. Many nights we could find Sugar stationed on the staircase, waiting for cars to come along and then jumping up in an effort to catch the light that flickered along that wall each time a car passed the house.

Sugar's happiness ended when, a year or two later, we acquired two kittens from the family of a junior high school friend of Laura. They had named one of the kittens Columbus, because he liked to explore things. This was about the time of the movie *Goodbye, Columbus*, with Ali MacGraw, and we named the other kitten Ali. At the time, the double entendre involved in Ali cat did not even occur to thickheaded me.

The two kittens were regarded as a major annoyance by Sugar, and their presence soon converted her into a grumpy and grouchy old woman. Until this time, I had never heard a cat growl, but Sugar did plenty of that now.

Fortunately for Sugar but unfortunately for the rest of us, Ali did not live very long. One evening after the kittens had been with us for just a few months, Laura came sobbing into the house and told me that Ali was lying in the street and not moving. He was indeed dead, but without a mark on him; so he hadn't been run over. As best I could figure it, Ali was sitting beside or in the street, saw the headlights of an oncoming car, jumped up to try to catch the moving beam of light, and suffered a fractured skull when hit by the car. I wish Ali had followed Sugar's system concerning headlights, instead of going after the real thing.

Columbus (or Bum, as I usually called him) survived his brother for quite a few years. I often played Pavlov with him when I was in the kitchen carving roast beef or some other delicacy for the family. My practice was to put a small piece of meat on top of one of the old shoes that I wore around the house (instead of messing up the floor by putting the meat on it). I would then point at the shoe, and Bum would come running to the shoe and gobble up the piece of meat. Originally he was, of course, attracted by the smell of the meat, but before long I could induce Bum to come running to me just by pointing at my shoe, even if I had not put a piece of meat on it. Of course, whenever Bum came running to a meatless shoe, I rewarded him with a piece of meat after all.

Bum was mostly an outdoors cat, and he hung around when I would pick the fruit off the sour cherry tree in the backyard. I was generally situated on a stepladder that I placed near the ends of branches, and Bum would sometimes climb the tree and then walk along a branch until he was out to where I was picking cherries, sometimes actually getting in the way. Imagine that…a cat getting in the way! At least there was no danger of me stepping on his tail in these situations.

Fritzi

Fritzi was a mixed-breed dog (spitz and cocker spaniel, I believe) that we acquired after Ali's death. For a number of years thereafter our household included Fritzi and the other two cats.

Sugar became ever more disgruntled, for in addition to the damn kittens we had now brought in a damn dog. However, Fritzi and Bum got along okay and sometimes teamed up when we happened to leave food unattended on the dining room table for a while. The game plan was for Bum to get up on the table and, in the course of taking a few samples for himself, knock some of the food onto the floor. This was, of course, where Fritzi was stationed, and she knew what to do with whatever fell her way.

Various dogs seem to regard some rather unusual food items as delicacies, and in Fritzi's case the delicacy of choice was lettuce. Perhaps she had somehow become aware that leafy green vegetables are better for the heart than are red meats.

Fritzi also liked chasing games, and the first floor of the house had a circular floor plan that was conducive to such games. Usually Fritzi would chase me (and, sometimes, one or another of the kids) round and round until I came to a stop in the kitchen and turned around to face her. I picked the kitchen as the stopping place because it had a tile floor, and Fritzi, while trying to stop herself, would go skidding across that floor.

Some of Nancy's Original Cats

In the course of talking about Manny, I've mentioned these other cats—especially Tiggy, with whom Manny fought, and Becky, with whom he played.

Another of the originals was Bozo, who was an ugly sonofabitch and very well named. He didn't like me, never blinked at me, and peed on my pillow now and then. I didn't like him, never blinked at him, and…you get the picture. However, Nancy tells me that Bozo was the only cat that Becky ever snuggled with.

Becky was a beautiful little tortoiseshell cat who was very private and standoffish. She was a lot like Sugar in that she pretty much didn't like anybody, animal or human. Except that Becky did like Nancy—and Bozo! All cats like Nancy. Even when Nancy is dining on her favorite food, salmon, generous portions of the same are allocated to the cats. Also, Nancy provides bottled water or filtered water to the cats as well as herself. I'm the only resident who takes it straight from the tap.

Becky's frequent practice, in the case of the other cats and me, was to hiss whenever one of us happened to walk past her. She tried to avoid such situations by spending as much time as possible in some nook or cranny where there would be very little cat or Daddy traffic passing by. Her favorite such spot was under the bottom shelf of a built-in bookcase on the lower level of our townhouse.

Becky's negative feeling toward me possibly originated one day when I walked into the apartment and closed the front door on her tail. Her screaming and yelling continued for the few seconds it took me to realize what had happened and to free her.

Becky would usually come running to the front door when she heard someone in the process of entering the apartment. She was eager to greet any newcomer who might possibly give her some more food. Becky was quite aggressive around the food dishes, and with multiple cats we did have multiple food dishes. She was generally the first to arrive when fresh food was put in the cat dishes and would start in on the contents of one of them. When another cat arrived and headed for another dish, Becky would often move over, shoulder the other cat out of the way, and start in on that other dish. It wasn't that Becky was bigger and stronger than the other cats—she was, in fact, the smallest. But in the food dish neighborhood, she was the pushiest and most aggressive.

Becky's pushiness cost her one time when I wasn't around to see the excitement. One day a big paper shopping bag was temporarily lying on the floor of the apartment, and curious Becky stuck her head inside the bag, probably in hopes that it contained food. On finding the bag empty, she withdrew her head but, in doing so, managed to put her head through one of the bag handles. Becky then proceeded to go berserk trying to rid herself of the darn thing. She tried to run away from this object to which she was attached, but the bag stayed with her over hill and dale. Nancy was in hot pursuit, trying desperately to catch up to Becky or corner her somewhere in order to remove the bag. After quite a chase, Nancy finally succeeded in cornering Becky under the bed in the spare room. Poor old

Becky was panting her little head off and wondering why this "monster bag" was pursuing her. Nancy gently rid her of the "monster."

In addition to being a tough guy, as he proved to Manny many times, Tiggy also was, in a way, the smartest cat I've ever seen. Nancy acquired him when he was a very small kitten, years before I was in the picture; and, virtually from the start, Tiggy displayed an aversion to cat food, and kindhearted Nancy got in the habit of feeding him chicken. I say that a cat who eats chicken every Sunday and Monday and Tuesday, etc., is a very smart cat. It soon became a routine for Nancy to cook a whole chicken, pick all the meat off the bones, store the meat in the refrigerator, and dole out some of it to Tiggy at each mealtime. Later, I got involved in the routine and sometimes did the chicken picking myself. I say a cat who maneuvers two humans into cooking and picking chickens so that the cat can have fresh chicken at each meal is a very smart cat indeed.

Ginger

Earlier I spoke of Ginger, or "the kitten," and of her youthful activities of playing with Manny and annoying all of the older cats. Ginger also played with Nancy and me, and our favorite game involved Ginger in fetching those small soft rubber balls, which are common cat toys. One of our traditions was to play this game after I got home from work and took off my workday shoes and placed them on the floor outside my closet upstairs. Nancy and I would station ourselves at the top of the stairs and take turns bouncing a ball down the staircase. Ginger would chase the ball down the stairs, pick it up in her mouth, and then race back up the stairs and deposit the ball in one of those shoes, which, of course, reeked with Essence of Daddy's Feet. This process was repeated until Nancy and I decided that we really did have other things that we ought to be doing.

Ginger purred frequently and very loudly. We believe she was probably the "purrest" kitten there ever was. Whenever Nancy or I reached down to pet Ginger, she would immediately start her loud purring. Often she would roll over on her back so that we could stroke her belly. At some point, Ginger developed a practice of joining me when I was working out on my rowing machine. She would often parade around and around the rowing machine as I was moving back and forth, and periodically she would lie down and roll over on her back so that I could stroke her belly.

Over the years, Ginger developed quite a belly. She was a very good jumper in her younger days, but later she had all she could do just to get up on an easy chair for one of her siestas. She weighed about fifteen pounds even though she had a rather small frame. We sometimes thought that we should change her name from Ginger to Doppelginger.

In part because of her weight and in part because of the effect of the spaying surgery on her abdominal muscles, Ginger had quite a floppo-flappo, a term Nancy and I coined for that part of Ginger's belly that sagged down, way down. Whenever Ginger walked or trotted, her floppo-flappo swung back and forth, so that when she was viewed from behind, it appeared that part of Ginger was moving forward and part of her was moving from side to side.

Ginger demonstrated that she was capable of purring and doing other things at the same time. When she was a little kitten, she had a habit, when one of us was holding her, of purring and at the same time giving forth with farts that were inaudible but detectable by one of the other senses. If she had not soon outgrown this habit, it would no doubt have become a rare occurrence for her to be picked up and held by her mommy or daddy.

As Ginger grew older, she became less receptive to the other cats bothering her or even coming near her and often hissed or growled at them. On many such occasions Ginger would be purring, perhaps because she was lying on the sofa next to Nancy, and would issue her hiss or growl without any interruption of her purring.

Whenever Ginger's mommy or daddy was in the kitchen slicing, cooking, or otherwise dealing with meat, one or more of the cats would be out there begging—and begging successfully. But usually not Ginger. Because she was old or fat or lazy (or all of the above), she would generally continue lying on her favorite easy chair in the living room. But when we looked into the living room, we could see Ginger's eyes boring holes into us and delivering the following summons: "Bring some meat to me here in the living room!" And we always did.

Ginger used a similar approach with another cat, by the name of Jazzy, who was a member of our household for a number of years. On numerous occasions when Ginger evidently wanted to lie on Nancy's chair, she would find Jazzy already lying there and would accordingly sit on the floor in front of the chair and stare up at Jazzy. Invariably, it wouldn't require a very long period of staring before Jazzy jumped off the chair and Ginger jumped on.

The Siblings

In spite of the fact that Nancy had so many cats over the years, she had never had two kittens at the same time until we acquired Woody and Annie from a shelter. Her interest in having two kitties at the same time was increased by my stories of the fun I had long ago watching Columbus and Ali play together as kittens.

When we set out for the shelter, our objective was to obtain two female kittens of approximately the same age. However, during our tour through the shelter looking at the kitties available for adoption, we spotted two newly arrived littermates, one of each gender. Nancy immediately fell in love with the female. And immediately thereafter, as she looked at the two kittens lying in the cage snuggled against one another, Nancy realized she couldn't bear to separate the little female from her brother. So we took both of them.

Annie, however, apparently decided that it was not a good idea to keep her and Woody together. Though for a time after they entered our household the two of them got along fine and spent time lying together on the sofa or an easy chair, they drifted apart as time passed. The main reason for this seemed to be Woody's inclination to rough up his sister from time to time. It got to the point where often a bed, a chair, a room, or whatever was not big enough for both of them, and Annie would leave when Woody arrived.

Nancy and I agreed that Annie, a pastel tortoiseshell, was the most beautiful cat we had ever seen and that Woody was a plain old orange tabby. However, Woody *really* liked Nancy. Most times when he heard Nancy's voice calling him, Woody put on his dog act and went running to where Nancy was. Sometimes when I was at home and Nancy was away for a while, Woody would wander through the house yowling. I think he was calling Nancy.

All of our cats spent some time in our bedroom upstairs lying on the bed, on a chair, on the clothes hamper by the window, or (particularly when the doorbell rang) under the bed. In her early days with us, Annie spent most of her time in the bedroom and seemed to be becoming more and more like Becky in that she preferred to keep to herself instead of near the other cats. Annie also became more like Becky in that she displayed a strong preference for Nancy and a distaste for having any dealings with me. Almost every time I reached down to pet or stroke her, she issued a protest that sounded like a cross between a meow and a growl. She protested more loudly on those occasions when I picked her up, even though my reason for picking her up was, almost invariably, to bring her to Nancy. But I dearly loved Annie despite the apparent absence of a reciprocal feeling on her part.

On most weekday mornings during the time period I am discussing, I got up before Nancy and often found that we had been sharing the bed with one or more cats, sometimes including Annie. On those mornings when Annie was not already on the bed, she was often on the clothes hamper or elsewhere in the bedroom and usually would come over and jump up on the bed just as I was leaving it. It seems that, although Annie liked to lie next to Nancy, sometimes she would forgo this pleasure until it no longer entailed being next to me as well.

I didn't have a problem with Nancy and Annie doting on one another, but I can't say the same for Woody. He seemed to feel that his position as number one was threatened whenever Nancy and Annie were together. Often when he heard Nancy talking to Annie, he gave the appearance of displaying jealousy by running from wherever he was in the house to wherever Nancy and Annie were and demanding equal (or, indeed, preferential) treatment. When this occurred, Woody's arrival was usually the signal for Annie's departure.

The Death of Becky

A number of years ago Becky died at the age of twenty-two, after having been a member of the household of, first, Nancy and her mother and, later, Nancy and me for a total of some twenty years. Although Becky was never one of Nancy's very favorite cats, she became more and more attached to her as Becky became older, more infirm, and more reclusive.

Becky's death was an overwhelmingly sad event, especially for Nancy, partly because of her love for Becky, partly because she had for so long been accustomed to having Becky around as a significant part of her life, and partly because of the struggle we went through to preserve Becky's life and make it reasonably bearable.

In the last months of Becky's life, her various afflictions associated with old age, including asthma and kidney problems, caused her to become very dehydrated. The veterinarian suggested that Becky would be more nearly comfortable if we hydrated her twice a day, and we accordingly did so for the last couple months of her life. The hydration was a very ticklish procedure and involved both Nancy and me. I did the easy part, holding Becky still with one hand and holding up the water bag with the other. Nancy had the tough job, inserting the needle through Becky's skin without drawing blood. Becky, of course, did not enjoy her role in any of this.

At some point it became apparent that we were fighting a losing battle and that Becky was suffering too much. It was time to put her down. But Nancy did not want to follow the traditional route of taking Becky to the animal hospital and having the deed done while Becky lay on one of those cold metal tables in one of those bleak little rooms. Nancy had learned of a vet who would come to the home, and we arranged for it to happen there.

The ceremony was planned by Nancy and took place on the lower level of our home, not far from Becky's favorite refuge under the bottom shelf of a built-in bookcase. The lights were low and candles were lighted at several places around the room. Some of Nancy's favorite music—a "Gymnopedie" by Erik Satie, "Adagio for Strings" by Samuel Barber, and "The Lark Ascending" by Ralph Vaughan Williams—was playing on the stereo. Nancy sat on the davenport holding Becky cradled in her arms, and I patted the beautiful shiny dark fur on the top of Becky's head. As the awful needle went into Becky's body, I gave utterance to a variation on a line from *Hamlet*: "Good night, sweet princess, and flights of angels sing thee to thy rest."

I expect that all this sounds quite maudlin to you, but I believe it is saved from that by reason of the sentiments being real and heartfelt. Nancy was crying throughout; I was doing plenty of sobbing by the end; and it was apparent that the veterinarian was also touched. Even to this day Nancy may be moved to shed tears when something reminds her of Becky. This can be hearing on the radio the start of any of the pieces of music aforementioned or seeing one of the other cats behave in a particular way like Becky used to behave.

Phoebe

At the time of Becky's death, we had no intention of acquiring another cat. However, coincidentally, later in the same month Nancy learned that a friend of hers was looking for a home for a six-month-old female kitten who had already been spayed. We couldn't pass up a deal like that, and so Phoebe joined our brood.

Phoebe, like Ginger, was a calico, though she had fewer black and tan markings than Ginger. Also like Ginger, she was quite a large cat and developed a floppo-flappo, though it was not as pronounced as Ginger's.

As seems to be common with kittens, Phoebe was quite aggressive toward the other cats when she entered our household. Unfortunately, she remained aggressive for a number of years and, in particular, drove Annie crazy by ambushing, chasing, and jumping her. This would have been a much bigger problem for Annie if the original veterinary activities with respect to Phoebe (before we acquired her) had not included the removal of her front claws.

The absence of front claws made Phoebe near unique among our cats, as did her apparent preference for me over Nancy, at least initially. I believe that Phoebe was the first cat to display love toward me. She sometimes liked to have me pick her up, cradle her in my arms, and snuggle her against my face, purring all the while (Phoebe, that is!). Often she would approach me and give forth a squeak to let me know she wanted some snuggling. On the other hand, if I picked her up and started snuggling without such an invitation, she was likely to give a squeak in order to let me know she would prefer to be back on the floor. Phoebe squeaked often enough to induce us to give her a nickname: Squeakheart.

Phoebe joined me in the bathroom sometimes, just as I was stepping out of the shower, and requested some snuggling. Of course, I couldn't refuse her. Visualize, if you will, this naked old man holding and snuggling a great big calico putty tat. On second thought, you'd probably rather skip the visualizing. I will say that those were one of the few occasions when I was just as glad that Phoebe didn't have front claws.

Sometimes when I was in bed at night, Phoebe would clamber onto me, put her head on my shoulder, and purr almost right into my ear. She also liked to lie between my legs when I was seated on the recliner chair, especially when I had leaned back so that the footrest had popped up. On many occasions when Phoebe was upstairs at the time when I settled into the easy chair and leaned back, the sound of that footrest popping up caused Phoebe to race down the stairs, issue a squeak as she reached the bottom, run across the living room, and hop up onto the chair and plant herself between my legs.

As time passed, Phoebe became more close to Nancy than was originally the case, and if Nancy left the living room, Phoebe would often jump down from her position between my legs on the recliner chair and follow Nancy. Also, Phoebe sometimes imitated Woody by running to Nancy in response to Nancy's call.

On those relatively few days during the year when neither the furnace nor the air conditioning was running, so that we could have windows open, the cats liked to sit at one window or another and look out at the world through the screen. (They also liked to look out a window when it was closed, but it was more fun when they could hear the outside world in addition to seeing it.) Sometimes Phoebe would be looking out a bedroom window when Nancy and I came in from the garage after shopping or whatever. We were able to see that she invariably greeted us with a series of squeaks and, if it was a nice day with the windows open, we could hear her greeting as well. She didn't then remain at the window, however. She had learned that when she saw us in the alley we would soon thereafter come in the front door, so she usually met us at the door to greet us again.

On those nice days when we could open up the house, we would often put a chair at the front door so that the cats could stand on it and look out through the screen, which constituted the upper half of the outside door. Sometimes there would be two cats on the chair (most often Woody and Phoebe), standing side by side with their hind feet on the chair seat and their front paws on the top of the chair back. Nancy and I much enjoyed watching the two cats standing thus, in what we have come to call a meerkat pose, and turning their heads in unison when a squirrel or something else outside caught their attention.

One morning Phoebe gained a nonfeline playmate, at least for a little while. This was Sparky, a crayfish fresh from Lake Michigan, who was a resident of one of Nancy's little aquariums for a couple of years. Sparky from time to time endeavored to get out of the aquarium and take a stroll. On the morning in question, as I came down the stairs, I noticed that Phoebe's attention was riveted on something in the front hall. Sure enough, on closer inspection, I saw that Sparky was taking a constitutional and Phoebe was keeping her company—but just looking, not touching. If Phoebe hadn't drawn my attention to the situation, Sparky might have got under some furniture and disappeared for the duration. (And, no, I don't remember how Nancy determined that Sparky was indeed a she.)

I spoke earlier about Nancy or me being joined by cats in the kitchen, and Phoebe certainly became the champion food beggar of the bunch. Her procedure, when a piece of meat was either dropped toward the floor for her or tossed in her direction, was either to try to catch the meat with her clawless front paws or try to bat it down. It seems as though she couldn't decide whether she wanted to be a wide receiver or a cornerback. In any event, neither of us has ever seen another cat behave in this manner.

Phoebe had several other traits that I think demonstrated her near uniqueness. Far more than any other cat I've run into, she would tolerate being petted by a foot, even a foot on which a slipper or shoe was being worn. If she happened to be lying on a chair that I happened to pick up to move somewhere else, she would continue lying on the chair during the move, instead of jumping off the chair as soon as I started to pick it up.

Also, if we started up a vacuum cleaner in Phoebe's vicinity, she would generally stay where she was instead of skedaddling the moment we turned it on. (And this was definitely not due to any deafness on Phoebe's part.) Speaking of vacuum cleaners, from time to time I would take the mattress and box spring off our bed so that I could vacuum up the cat fur on the carpet under the bed. One time when I did this I found Phoebe still lying under the bed. I can't imagine any other cat continuing to lie there while a mattress and then a box spring are raised up and flipped off the bed frame and then flopped on the floor. Phoebe's handling of the aforesaid flipping and flopping helped to demonstrate for me that she may have been the most unflappable of all cats and that she had surpassed Ginger as my favorite pet ever.

Elmer

This fellow (or gal) was a fish who was a denizen of one of Nancy's aquariums. At some point Elmer became ill or was injured and spent much of the time either lying at the bottom of the aquarium or swimming around upside down. This presented an occasion for Nancy to display, for the umpteenth time, her great love for animals. In an effort to save Elmer, she put the fish in a large fish bowl all by himself and with his own personal air stone and frequent changes of water. She even went so far as to pet Elmer from time to time.

All ultimately in vain. Though Elmer hung on for a while and sometimes was able to swim around in the more customary manner, he died after spending about a month in his private bowl.

Postscript

No, that's not the name of another animal. As a matter of fact, the little story I want to relate here has nothing to do with any pet of ours. It has to do with somebody else's pet, and I think it's rather funny—at least from our point of view.

A while back, a little dog (possibly belonging to our next-door neighbor's girlfriend) stayed in his unit for a number of days. The neighbor's practice concerning this dog, at least some of the time, was to let the dog out on the back patio instead of taking it for a walk. His practice also included nonuse of a pooper scooper, and the inevitable result was the accumulation of various piles of dog turds on the little patio.

Nancy asked the neighbor on more than one occasion to remedy the situation, to no avail. She accordingly then took matters into her own hands and relocated the accumulation of poop to our neighbor's back stoop. Actually, I shouldn't say Nancy took matters into her own hands because, in truth, she used the turner or spatula that was hanging on the neighbor's charcoal grill on the patio. Naturally, upon completing the operation, Nancy put the utensil back where she had found it. We have no information as to whether our neighbor thereafter noticed any difference in the taste of his hamburgers or other grilled meats!

Chapter 25

Meesh-i-gan!

Prior to starting in law school at the University of Michigan in Ann Arbor, I had been a reasonably avid fan of college football in general but not an ardent fan of any particular team. Because I'm from Big Ten country, I most closely followed the fortunes of Big Ten teams. As a matter of fact, during my college years at a university that was by no means a football powerhouse, I didn't attend a single game but instead would often, on a Saturday afternoon, listen to a Big Ten game on the radio.

Things became more focused when I started law school. I became a Michigan fan and remain such to this day. However, I'm not one of those who drives a pennant-and-sign-bedecked van to all of the games, home and away. When it comes to signs on the car, our style (Nancy being quite an animal lover) was a bumper sticker depicting little furry creatures and captioned "Give Them a Brake." However, because bumper stickers tend to unstick and curl up, ours for some time seemed to bear the caption "Give Them a Bra."

A colleague of mine at Martin, Barton & Fargo in the early days was one of those Michigan football fans who drove up to Ann Arbor for all of the home games. The process whereby he became a fan followed a different path than in my case. He was from Ohio, went to college at Ohio State, and remained an Ohio State football fan throughout his three years in law school at Michigan. Somehow he was transformed into a Michigan fan after graduating from law school!

While I was in law school, I, of course, went to all of the home football games, and, after our marriage following my freshman year, Barbara went to the games with me. One of the favorite parts of the experience for both of us was the Michigan marching band, especially the way the band members came *running* onto the field in marching order, while playing their instruments, in response to the band director's pregame direction: "Band...take the field!"

Ever since my law school days, I have followed Michigan's football fortunes by listening to and/or watching virtually all of Michigan's football games on radio and/or television. Radio was my main reliance for all the years that passed before so many college football games began to be carried on television. Luckily, the Chicago area being just across the lake from Michigan, I could pick up all the games on a University of Michigan football network station in Benton Harbor–St. Joseph. Most Saturday afternoons during football season I would manage to stay home and listen to the games on the Michigan network station, whether I was in the house or outdoors raking leaves, painting, or whatever.

For many years the Michigan network play-by-play broadcaster was a fellow named Bob Ufer. He was apparently a very rabid Michigan fan, and the two of us suffered through a lot of lean years together before Bo Schembechler took over as coach. The way Bob Ufer pronounced the name of the university when he was being dramatic, which was often, has furnished my chapter title.

In more recent years, when so many college football games (including, luckily for me, almost every Michigan game) are televised on a network, cable, or satellite station, my practice for several years was to watch the Michigan game with the audio off and to listen to the Michigan football network radio broadcast. However, at some point when I tuned in the Benton Harbor–St. Joseph station to listen to the Michigan game, I found that the voices of the broadcasters were unfamiliar. From comments made by them and from announcements made during station breaks concerning changes in the station's format, I soon gleaned the very disturbing information that the station had switched from the Michigan football network to the Notre Dame football network. Ugh!

One of my favorite Michigan games ever was the Rose Bowl game of 1993, when Tyrone Wheatley ran wild for Michigan and Mark Brunell seemed to throw one touchdown pass after another for Washington, with Michigan coming out on top in a close, high-scoring game.

A game that I didn't like nearly as much was the Michigan-Colorado game sometime in the mid-1990s. This was the game where Kordell Stewart, the Colorado quarterback, threw a long Hail Mary pass into the end zone on the last play of the game and a Colorado wide receiver caught the pass to win the game after the ball had been tipped around a bit by players from both teams. I have been reminded of this dreadful game a few times because that final play has periodically been included in highlights from past games that have been shown as lead-ins to telecasts of college football.

What I've never been able to understand about Hail Mary situations at the end of a game is why the defensive backs try to intercept the pass, with the result that the ball gets tipped around and possibly ends up in the wrong hands. Why don't the defenders just bat down the goddamn thing?

There were, of course, Michigan football games that I did not watch or listen to because of other commitments, and one such occasion is memorable because of something that my son Ed did. On the day of the Michigan–Ohio State game one year, Barbara and I were in attendance at Parents' Day or some equivalent doings at Miami University in Ohio, where our other son, Tom, was a student. Ed watched or listened to the game, kept track of every play, and later surprised me with a typewritten transcript giving a complete play-by-play account of the game. And, better yet, Michigan had won. It was especially nice of Ed to do this because at the time he was a student at the University of Illinois, had become a fan of Illinois football, and usually paid no attention to Michigan games.

I raised my children to be Michigan football fans but, as just indicated, Ed became a turncoat when he went to college at Illinois. Tom has been able to remain a Michigan fan as well as a Miami University fan, inasmuch as the two schools rarely compete against one another (except in hockey). For a number of years now Tom has lived in Mishawaka, Indiana, right next door to South Bend and, thus, in the heart of Notre Dame country. Tom has had the fortitude to maintain and display his Michigan loyalty in that hostile environment and is also raising his boys right.

Tom is probably the only one of my children who is still a Michigan football fan, for I expect that my daughters are not into college football at this late date. Laura, however, is the only one of my kids who is actually a

Michigander (or is it Michigoose?), having been born in Ann Arbor during my senior year.

Most of you will probably be glad for a digression from Michigan football for a moment during which I will mention that what happened to the place where Laura, Barbara, and I lived in Ann Arbor may epitomize what often happens in areas immediately adjacent to large and expanding universities and other institutions. We lived in one of the apartments located in what was originally a single-family residence just a block away from the law school and right across the street from the graduate school of business.

The first time the three of us were back in Ann Arbor after I graduated, Barbara took a picture of Laura and me sitting on the front steps of the house. After the lapse of some period of time we were again in Ann Arbor and wanted to go by the house. We couldn't do it. No house—yes parking lot. After the lapse of another period of time, we were back again and found that the street on which we had lived had itself disappeared because that area had been incorporated into the campus.

Back to football. Although Ohio State and Michigan State are no doubt the main football rivals of Michigan, the rivalries with Illinois and Iowa have played a more significant role in my own Michigan football experience. For a number of years after Ed graduated from Illinois, he and I attended the Illinois-Michigan game each year, either in Champaign or Ann Arbor.

The only away game that I saw while I was in law school was the game at Illinois during my freshman year. Michigan was a heavy favorite, but Illinois won. Illinois has had a history of frequently upsetting heavily favored Michigan teams. But not always. During the early years of the Schembechler coaching regime at Michigan, I was listening to a University of Illinois football network broadcast of an Illinois-Michigan game, which Michigan was leading something like 40–0, when I heard the Illinois broadcaster complain, "We haven't even scored on these guys in three years."

An Illinois-Michigan game which I didn't watch or listen to occurred while Barbara and I were at Daytona Beach for a short vacation. During that Saturday afternoon, I heard that Illinois was ahead 21–7 during the first half, but I heard no more about the game until the next day, when I learned that Michigan had scored the next 65 points.

Michigan's enormous comeback in that game was a subject of discussion several years later during an Illinois-Michigan game in Ann Arbor, which I was attending with a couple of friends. At a point when Illinois was ahead during the first half something like 10–7, one of my friends, a young guy who was an Illinois graduate, wanted to make a bet as to whether Michigan would also win this game by at least fifty points. I, of course, wouldn't make such a silly bet, particularly because he wouldn't give me any decent odds. However, once again there was an avalanche of Michigan points during the rest of the game—I should have made the bet.

The Michigan-Iowa rivalry became significant to me during law school because of my friendship with a classmate by the name of Howie. He was one of the best guys I've ever known but was also from Iowa, a graduate of the University of Iowa, and an ardent Iowa fan. Howie was in the group of us that sat together at Michigan home games. In all three years we were in law school, the Michigan-Iowa game was played in Ann Arbor, and in each of the first two years Iowa led 13–7 in the second half. However, in both games Michigan came back to win 14–13. In our senior year, Iowa was ahead 21–13 at the end of the third quarter, and Howie was exultant that this time, at last, Iowa had the extra point in hand. But again victory for Iowa was not to be. Michigan threw two long touchdown passes in the fourth quarter and won 27–21.

A much less pleasant Michigan-Iowa game, for me, was played at Iowa City years later, in 1985, I believe. At that time Iowa was ranked the top college football team in the country and Michigan was ranked second; so it was a *big* game. Unfortunately, I was scheduled to take a business trip on that Saturday, to Ann Arbor of all places, to meet with a client at his home. I flew to Detroit early that morning, the client met me at the airport, and we went to his home for our meeting. Luckily, the football game wasn't very far along when our business was concluded and the client was also interested in Michigan football; so we watched the game while we lunched and until the time came for me to get to the airport for my flight back to Chicago.

While the client drove me to the airport, we listened to the game on the car radio; but I figured I would be out of luck, gamewise, once I arrived at the airport and boarded the plane. On a short flight, like from Detroit to Chicago, the airlines never showed movies or anything else on the big screen in the plane. Except on special occasions—and it turned out that this was a special occasion, at least for planes flying out of the Detroit airport. The game was on the big screen all the way back to Chicago.

The game was not quite over when we landed at O'Hare airport; so I disembarked as quickly as possible and hustled to one of the airport bars. I arrived there just in time…just in time to see Iowa kick a field goal in the final seconds to win the game 12–10.

As you may know, Michigan's football fortunes in recent years have not been fortunate. I will therefore say no more on the subject, except to express my hope that we are about to reach a turning point.

Chapter 26

Classical Music

During my childhood, my father regularly listened to several classical music programs: the Voice of Firestone, the Bell Telephone Hour, and a program sponsored by Cities Service. At that time, I had no interest in or liking for classical music. Later on, when my views had changed, I realized that there were pieces of classical music that I had unwittingly enjoyed even during my childhood, in the themes of some of my favorite radio programs: Mussorgsky on *Escape*, Sibelius on *I Love a Mystery*, Rossini and Liszt on *The Lone Ranger*, Saint-Saens on *The Shadow*, and Gounod (I think it was) on *The Fat Man*.

In my adult years I started listening to classical music in order to have a pleasant background at the office with few interruptions for commercials. Over the years the commercials became more frequent, but I continued to listen to classical music both at the office and at home. Originally I was most interested in symphonic-type music, but there were specific incidents later that kindled interest in chamber music and classical vocal music.

My daughter Gail played the violin when she was a teenager, and her teacher was a graduate student in music at a nearby university. Her violin teacher's graduate recital was an event that Gail was expected to and desired to attend, and I was elected to accompany her. I trace my liking for chamber music to this time, for I much enjoyed a couple of solo violin pieces, a sonata for piano and violin, and Ravel's string quartet.

In the case of vocal classical music, the turning point was a program I was listening to on the car radio while I was en route to do some shopping. When I arrived at my destination I was listening to the *Four Last Songs* written by Richard Strauss and sung by Elisabeth Schwarzkopf. This music was so breathtakingly beautiful that I just sat in my parked car and listened until it was over.

The interest in vocal music that was sparked by the long-ago radio program encompasses opera as well as songs and lieder. Nancy shares my interest in opera and other classical music, and I understand that her interest was triggered by the soundtrack of the movie *Barry Lyndon*. She has long been quite a fan of Placido Domingo and was thrilled a number of years ago when I secured tickets for second row seats for a production of Giuseppe Verdi's *Otello*. These tickets had been turned back to the box office because the original purchaser was unable to attend; by a stroke of luck I arrived at the box office just at the time when the tickets became available for resale. Unfortunately, the tragedy of the Mexico City earthquake intervened, and Domingo had to cancel his appearance in the opera and proceed to Mexico City instead, inasmuch as members of his family resided in that area. Nancy and I still attended the opera, but Domingo's absence and the reason for his absence put something of a damper on the occasion.

Chapter 27

Mr. Fun

When Warren and I first met, he was in eighth grade and I was a freshman in high school. Although we ended up in the same high school class, I was one semester ahead of him and, thus, was in the first semester of ninth grade when he was in the second semester of eighth grade. At that time I was participating in debate as an extracurricular activity, and one of my assignments was to coach an eighth-grade debate team at the grade school Warren attended. Warren was one of the eighth-graders who signed up for that team and subjected himself to my coaching.

Though I have no memory as to Warren's proficiency as a debater nor as to my proficiency as a coach, I do have a distinct recollection of my appearance at the grade school to give a talk to the eighth-grade class members for purposes of interesting them in debate and persuading some of them to sign up for the team. My instructions concerning this recruiting trip were to check in at the grade school principal's office so that she could escort me to the eighth-grade classroom and introduce me to the teacher and students. Although this was indeed the way it worked out, I had initially found that the principal was not in her office when I arrived at the school. After I sat down and waited for a time, the principal appeared, apologized for keeping me waiting, and took me to the eighth-grade classroom.

The school principal had an explanation as to why there had been a delay in her arriving at her office to meet me. She said that she had asked one of the pupils at the school whether there was a high school boy waiting in her office and had been told that there was no high school boy but that a sixth-grader was sitting in her office. It was, of course, not pleasant to learn that someone mistook me for a sixth-grader, and it was even more bothersome to me that the school principal felt it necessary or appropriate to inform me that such a mistake had been made. I was thirteen years old at the time, and these were the days when my eleven-year-old sister was almost as tall as I. In addition to being little, I was also (evidently) not otherwise particularly imposing in appearance.

Warren and I knew each other ever since the brief period when I was his debate coach. We saw each other from time to time during high school days but never hung around together until near the end of my senior year, when I started running around with Warren and his beer-drinking buddies, who included Mort and Ed. During several years thereafter, I spent many evenings with Warren and these other guys, drinking beer and otherwise wasting time. Mort, by the way, lived across the street from the other side of the old cemetery from where I had lived as a young boy, and I had accordingly first known of him as being one of the Others.

Most of what our group of guys did in our late teens and early twenties has become firmly lodged in my forgettory, but I do remember one weekend when a bunch of us headed down to a state park about seventy miles away, beer, hamburgers, sweet corn, sleeping bags, etc., in tow. After helping ourselves to a few melons from a flatbed truck not far from the park entrance, we had our cookout at the park. For me the most exciting part of the evening was my effort, making use of a rusty old hatchet I had brought along, to chop wood for the fire after I had imbibed a number of bottles of beer. Luckily, I didn't chop anything other than wood.

The next morning, Warren favored us with his impression of the guy who had done number two in the old cemetery years before. However, Warren did not wish to limit himself to leaves and weeds for clean-up purposes. Instead, he requested that Mort hand him the magazine or newspaper of which Mort had taken possession. I can still visualize the scene that followed: Mort moving around and holding the paper goods just out of Warren's reach, as Warren tried to pursue him while remaining in a squatting position with his pants down.

As time passed, such doings of our old gang were interrupted, and eventually superseded, by college, military service, marriages, moves out of town, etc. (When I say "such doings," I'm not referring to egestion, which of course continued, but to our gang of guys running around together.)

All of the other guys were in the military, including four years in the Navy for Warren. I am unusual for someone in my age group, in that I was never in the military service, being deferred for a time as a student and, later on, as a father. For part of the time I was in college, Warren was stationed at a Navy post in New Jersey. During this period, he came up to New England to visit me one weekend. I assume we drank some beer, but the one thing I definitely remember us doing was going to see one of the great movies, *A Place in the Sun*.

During our adult years, Warren and I, and our wives, kept in pretty close and frequent touch (figuratively speaking). Many of my good times have occurred when Warren was present, and I found that his presence pretty much guaranteed that I was going to have a good time. I think this is due in large part to his combination of aplomb, laidbackness, and joie de vivre. In a word (hyphenated though it be), Warren was super-mellow. At any rate, as far as I'm concerned, Warren richly deserved the appellation of Mr. Fun.

The close relationship between Warren and me as adults began when I was his best man at his wedding to his first wife in her hometown in southern Illinois. He had asked two or three of the other guys in our group, but for one reason or another none of them could make the wedding. For a number of years after their marriage, Warren and his wife, Kay, lived outside the Chicago area, in Alton and Freeport, Illinois, and North Muskegon, Michigan. Barbara and I saw them from time to time but naturally saw them much more often when they moved to a Chicago suburb about nine years after they got married.

We visited them just once during the brief time they lived in Alton, when we stopped in on our way back from a vacation trip to the Smoky Mountains. While we were in Alton, a goose (nonfeathered variety) put Kay in the emergency room at the hospital. Evidently Warren and Kay had developed a playful practice of goosing one another from time to time, and this particular goose was administered by Kay to Warren when he sat down next to her. The goose caused Warren to rare up, and the back of his head happened to catch Kay just above her left eye, opening a nasty gash. When we took her to the emergency room for stitches, I don't know what account Warren provided the hospital personnel as to the cause of Kay's injury; but I do know that the apparent wife beater was the recipient of some skeptical looks.

Barbara and the kids and I visited Warren and his family once in a while in the several other towns where they lived, but for the most part they came to our place. We developed some pleasant traditions; for example, our families partook of many Thanksgiving dinners together. Warren's departure for home after a visit was always a letdown for me—as his car pulled away from our house on a Sunday afternoon, my feeling would invariably be that the fun was over for now and that I would be back at Martin, Barton & Fargo the next day.

Warren was such a cool guy that he was a source of fun even when he fell asleep. Sometimes he would take a nap on the sofa during a visit, and sometimes I would take this occasion to tie him up and/or pile various items on top of him. This, of course, had nothing to do with bondage and discipline, but it gave me something to do while he napped. On occasion, some of my kids helped in the project, and later Nancy became my accomplice. Everybody got a bang out of anticipating Warren's reaction when he awakened from his nap and saw what we had done. However, Warren always disappointed us by the lack of concern that he displayed when he awakened and became aware of his circumstances.

Somewhere along the line we had a get-together at our house when our friend Jack (who lived in New Jersey at the time) came back home for a visit to family and friends. Warren and Ed and their wives came over. Those two gentlemen had such a good time with John Barleycorn that evening that they ended up stripping down to their skivvies and romping around in the portable plastic wading pool that we had in the backyard for the kids.

Probably a couple of years after Warren crawled out of the wading pool, he and Kay and Barbara and I spent a weekend in Chicago together, staying in adjacent rooms at a lakefront motel. Our Friday night plans were dinner at a nice restaurant on the near north side, followed by a play at a downtown theater and a stop at the Gaslight Club, Warren having borrowed a key for this private club from some business associate of his. Naturally, all of this was prefaced by drinks at the motel. Unfortunately, Warren consumed three martinis at the motel and, when he added a fourth before dinner at the restaurant, he was gone, man. We had all we could do to keep him from immersing his head in the food on his plate. The rest of the evening proceeded as planned, though you no doubt couldn't prove it by Warren.

The next day's program included a couple of movies, lunch and dinner at two more nice restaurants, and a late-night stop at an establishment on Rush Street, which featured go-go dancers. (I don't know whether such establishments still exist—I get around even less nowadays than I used to.) We were seated right next to the small stage where the dancers did their gyrations, and from where I was sitting, I needed to turn my chair around a bit in order to view the dancing. For a time I did not do so but pretty much had my back to the stage while I was facing, and conversing with, the other three members of our party. Suddenly, I felt a hand on each side of my head, exerting a mild pressure to turn my head so that I was facing the stage. The young lady who was exerting that pressure had been performing a dance for the customers, including me, and evidently felt that it behooved each of the customers to pay attention to her performance.

On Sunday we took in one more movie and then headed to our respective suburban homes. We thought it had been a great weekend and agreed that we wanted to make it an annual event. However, as things so often seem to work out, it never happened again. And two or three years later the marriage of Warren and Kay ended.

A few years after his divorce, Warren got married again. This marriage lasted for a number of years, but then Warren and his second wife also split up. As I understand it, she walked out one January Sunday while Warren was watching the Super Bowl. Evidently he hardly glanced away from the television set as she left, but he claims that he thought she was going shopping or to run other errands. I have suggested to him that she was undoubtedly carrying more luggage than is customary in the case of shopping or running other errands.

Sometime after Warren became a single man again, I became the husband of Nancy. Several times she set up blind dates for Warren with friends of hers, and I pitched in once myself, lining him up to have cocktails with the young lady who happened to be my barber at the time. Warren also dated other women whom he met in one way or another, including a professional cellist whom he met through a dating service. They went out together several times, and she always brought along her valuable cello. I'm sure that Warren handled the omnipresence of the cello, and the difficulties of maneuvering it into and through restaurants, etc., with his usual savoir faire. However, the grouping of mellow, cello, and cellist proved once again that three's a crowd, and Warren's single status remained undisturbed.

During these years Nancy often referred to Warren as our social director, for he had introduced us to restaurants, jazz and other music venues, etc., with which we were previously unacquainted. A visit the three of us made to one new restaurant turned out to be a rare instance of Warren running out of mellowness. We took seats at the bar while we waited (and waited...and waited) for a table to become available. Because of the crowded conditions, it was necessary for me to sit on a stool next to the area of the bar, marked off by a set of railings, where the waitresses came to place drink orders and to return used glasses, trays, etc.

It wasn't long before the accumulation of used glasses and trays was such that some of the waitresses began placing these items on the bar right in front of me. This struck me as inappropriate, so I complained. I don't recall all of the details of the escalating series of events that led up to our departure from the restaurant. I believe some dirty dishes were moved hither and yon, and I know that each and every recipient of my complaints gave me a basic "Up your geekie" response. When we decided to walk out, I further expressed my displeasure by dropping or throwing my glass into the trash can that was also conveniently located near where I was seated. (What a he-man!) Warren's reaction was more violent—he dropped his glass on the tile floor, with a predictable result. His mellowness evidently could be exhausted under certain circumstances.

When Warren dated a friend of Nancy's, she and I generally went along, at least on the first date. The last instance of Nancy's matchmaking involved a friend of hers whom I'll call Peg. At that time Warren, as well as Nancy and I, lived in Chicago, and Peg lived in a western suburb; the plan was that he would pick up Peg and bring her back into town so that the four of us could go out to dinner at a snazzy French restaurant. Evidently Peg was not a habitué of the social whirl and felt it necessary to fortify herself to face an evening out with Warren. Thus, when Warren arrived at her home, he found that Peg had pretty much already completed a tour of the Barleycorn circuit. What to do? Obviously, what was next called for, at least according to Peg, was a stop for a drink at a watering hole on the way into Chicago to pick up Nancy and me.

By the time we linked up with Warren and Peg that evening, Peg was totally sloshed. We went ahead to the French restaurant anyway and found that it was not only snazzy but snooty—the waiter really looked down his nose at me when I tried to order Chianti (smooth!). During our meal, my focus was less on my food and more on doing what I could to avoid having Peg break glassware or crockery or burn herself with her cigarette.

After dinner we headed for a little club that was so located that we needed to do some walking from the garage where Warren had parked the car. Peg was having a terrible time walking and was convinced that this was a result of ill-fitting shoes. It was with difficulty that Nancy talked her out of throwing her shoes away and proceeding in stocking feet.

When we ultimately arrived at our destination, we were given two seats at the bar and two more just behind those two, so the two of us sitting at the bar swiveled our stools around and the four of us ended up more or less facing one another. Here again the focus was on Peg, not on the entertainment, drinks, or anything else, mainly because of the way Peg kept moving her lighted cigarette around. I had to change the position of my legs continuously in order to avoid having that lighted cigarette come in contact with my trousers, as we sat facing one another and as Peg gestured, gesticulated, and otherwise waved around her cigarette.

We weren't at that club very long before it became even more apparent that it was time that we got Peg home. We did so but, of course, at Peg's insistence, had to come in for a nightcap. In my case, Peg served red wine and, literally, filled my glass to overflowing. Peg is a nice woman, and it's a shame that her predate effort to bolster herself led to results which she never anticipated—and which she no doubt will never recall.

Warren and I were both very interested in geography, though our foci were not the same. For example, I am intrigued by the fact that many major rivers in the U.S.A. and elsewhere do indeed flow north. Warren, on the other hand, was very interested in railroads and urban transportation systems; he could describe the routes of many of the bus lines in Chicago.

In my later years as a sometime jogger, I generally did my jogging solo. At some point I decided to cover a different segment of the Prairie Path each weekend. This entailed parking my car at a place where a street or road was crossed by the path, running one and a half or two miles down the path to another such intersection, turning around and running back to the car, and then starting at that next intersection the following weekend. I knew that Warren had no interest in jogging, on the Prairie Path or anywhere else, but later on I asked him if he would like to drive around with me to see at least the starting points of my various jogging expeditions along the Prairie Path. Warren, being the railway man that he was, might have been the only person on earth who would have accepted such an invitation; he was interested in seeing the present condition of the streets and roads at the places where, years earlier, they had been crossed by the long-abandoned electric railway.

The last job that Warren held involved periodic trips by air, and on one of these trips he struck up a conversation with the fellow sitting next to him. It turned out that this guy, like Warren, had been born and raised in Elgin, Illinois, and that this guy, like Warren, had a friend named Gabler. Warren was speaking to the man who had been Rod's best friend all through grade school and high school. Once again, a small world.

For a number of his later years, Warren suffered from some hearing loss. This became an additional reason why he would frequently request that someone speaking to him repeat what had been said. In the case of Warren and me, I think there had been kind of a history of him pretending not to hear or not paying attention to the important things, if any, which I had to say from time to time. However, it became clear at some point that Warren also had a hearing problem. At first he had one bad ear, and he liked to say that he preferred to sit in a position where I would be on the side of his bad ear. Ultimately, he needed to get hearing aids, for one ear at first, as I recall, and later for the other as well.

Somewhere along the line, Warren also came to be afflicted with a short-term memory problem. This became accentuated as time passed and the disease progressed, and his family and friends came to recognize that his forgetfulness and confusion were such that he could no longer live alone and take care of himself. Accordingly, he took up residence in a retirement home in the Chicago suburbs, where he could receive the care he needed.

Throughout the development of his hearing and memory problems, Warren maintained his good humor and mellowness. He cracked jokes about his problems from time to time and, once in a while, still pretended not to hear when he did hear or pretended not to recall when he did remember. As far as I'm concerned, Warren continued to be mellow, a joy to be with, and Mr. Fun.

Before he moved into the retirement home, Warren came to our home now and then; he would often fall asleep during the evening, just like in the old days. We could tell he was asleep when he was sitting in an easy chair and his head gradually tilted forward until his chin touched his chest. However, I hasten to add, we didn't tie him up anymore.

For years after Warren moved into the retirement home, I visited him there on a fairly regular basis and for the first two or three years also took him to one park or another to walk and/or sit and to one sports bar or another to sit and have a beer.

Postscript

Warren died in May 2007.

Chapter 28

America's Bank

A long time ago I had a checking account at the Bank of America, which one day I decided I would close. From time to time during my adult years, I have moved my checking account from one bank to another, because of either dissatisfaction with the bank where the account was then located or incentives offered by another bank or both.

In any event, I went to a Bank of America location in Chicago, signed the paperwork I was told would be needed to close the account, and received a check in the amount of the current balance. I don't recall my reason for closing that particular account, but I do remember that plenty of dissatisfaction with the Bank of America ensued after that account was, as I thought, closed.

For three or four months, I received a monthly statement from the bank indicating that I had been charged a penalty for not maintaining a required minimum balance in the account. This required another visit to a Bank of America location, where I was able to get the penalties canceled and the account successfully closed, leaving me with a resolve not to do business with the Bank of America in the future.

Some years later, after I had moved my checking account from a bank I don't remember to LaSalle National Bank, I learned that I was back with Bank of America, inasmuch as it had acquired LaSalle. Because I then had no current reason for dissatisfaction with the Bank of America, I let the account remain where it was.

However, after the lapse of another period of, I believe, several years, I ran into big trouble at the Bank of America. In connection with making an installment payment of estimated federal income tax, I liquidated an investment and took the proceeds check to a Bank of America location to deposit it in my checking account so as to cover the check I would be writing to the Internal Revenue Service. This deposit was being made prior to the time when banks began requiring a customer to swipe his bank-issued debit card when making a deposit.

When I presented the proceeds check, which I had endorsed "For Deposit Only," and the teller had inquired as to my account number, I told him I did not know offhand, the deposit was made, and I went on my way. Some time thereafter I received a Bank of America statement, relating to the credit card it had issued to me long before, showing that the "For Deposit Only" check had been applied to the credit card account instead of being deposited in my checking account!!

At about the same time, I received a monthly bank statement relating to the checking account, which showed, of course, that the check I had written to the IRS, on account of our estimated income tax, did not clear. Soon thereafter I received a communication from the IRS, which showed—again of course—that I had failed to make a timely or adequate payment on account of our estimated tax and that I accordingly owed a penalty and interest.

Naturally I felt like the proverbial fly that sat on a toilet seat and got pissed off. However, the IRS was nice enough to waive the penalty when it received my explanation of how my tax payment came to be inadequate. Also, Bank of America recognized the need for it to reimburse me for the interest charged by the IRS.

I did not have any further problems with Bank of America subsequent to the episode just described, but Nancy and I recently moved our checking account to another bank because of inducements offered by that bank, including its sponsorship of telecasts of Chicago Blackhawks hockey games!

Chapter 29

Feline Transitions and Updates

As you may have suspected, there is one significant fact I have not mentioned relating to all of the pets (cats or otherwise) I have referred to in the preceding pages—namely, all of them have gone to the great beyond. Notably, Ginger died on February 17, 2003; Annie in the early days of December 2009; and Phoebe during the wee hours of January 29, 2013.

The death of Phoebe was especially agonizing for me because I should have been present at her side but was not. My feelings since that time have accordingly included guilt as well as grief.

Phoebe had been suffering from some unidentified illness and was scheduled for a return visit to the veterinarian on the next day, at which time she was to receive an additional medication, which I and, as I thought, the vet were optimistic concerning the result. Nancy, not being a cockeyed optimist like me, sat with Phoebe for hours and sometime around 3 a.m. awakened me with the devastating news. I shed tears again as I wrote the foregoing.

Nancy and I are still cat owners and have five at this time. Of the current cats in our household, we have had Mandy and Mooch for the longest time. They are black and white short-haired cats with "tuxedo" markings; they moved in about thirteen months after Ginger's death, at which time they were about eight months old.

Appendix C to this book was prepared by Nancy, is entitled "A Tale of Two Kitties," and describes how and why Nancy managed to add Mandy and Mooch to our household.

Another cat now in our household is an elderly female, black (with a few white patches), who arrived around 2008 and was given the name Lilith. She and I have never hit it off and have very little to do with one another, but she spends a lot of time on Nancy's lap and is much loved by Nancy—and also by my daughter Laura.

We had had very good luck with calico cats (Ginger and Phoebe), and this inspired Nancy to mention at the vet's office, several months after Phoebe's death, that we might be interested in taking in a calico kitten in the event an opportunity to do so arose. One of the women on the vet's staff advised Nancy that she was aware that such a kitten was currently available, and this led us to acquire Sophie, with whom we promptly fell head over heels in love.

Sophie was about thirteen weeks old at the time and had a beautiful coat with a lot more black and brown than either Ginger or Phoebe. The only blemish on her beauty is a patch of black fur on one side of her white throat, and I like to kid her about her goatee. Sophie's tail is relatively short and is not nearly as expressive as the tail of Phoebe, who Nancy often said had the world's greatest tail.

Sophie is interested in everything going on at our home and wants to participate in it all. For example, when I sit at the kitchen table with papers piled in front of me relating to lawyer work, memoirs, or bill payments, Sophie jumps onto the table and lies down on one or another pile of papers.

Ginger and Phoebe used to follow a similar routine, but their object was to grab my pen, which I repeatedly stuck out from one point or another of the pile of papers. My objective, on the other hand, was to pull the pen out of the cat's reach and thrust it out again from a different point in the pile of papers. This game was, of course, similar to the game we played with Manny years before with the plastic band on the staircase.

Sophie doesn't need the enticement of a pen being repeatedly proffered and then withdrawn. She is content just to lie down on the table near where her human daddy is sitting.

Sophie also displays her love for her human parents by kisses—for example, licking their hands. Also, on many mornings Sophie jumps on my bed and gives me a good licking to encourage me to wake up and feed her.

All in all, within a matter of months after entering our household, Sophie had become my favorite pet of all time. You may think me fickle, but I think that I, along with Nancy, was very fortunate to have encountered and loved three wonderful calico kittens. Nancy and I have also speculated as to whether Phoebe might have arranged, with any powers that may be, to have Sophie enter our household.

Our fifth cat is an orange tabby, who apparently was abandoned and then was rescued by us and made a part of our household in August 2015, when he was about five months old. His name is Toby, and he seems to be fitting in very well.

Chapter 30

Philosophizing

The courses I took during my freshman year in college included not only the accelerated chemistry course previously mentioned but also an introductory course in philosophy, which I took partly for the hell of it and partly because, at Rod's urging, I had read Will Durant's *Story of Philosophy* not long before. During that school year, while my interest in science ebbed as I floundered in the quagmire of Chemistry 2, my interest in philosophy soared as I became more intrigued by that introductory course. Before the year was over, I had decided that my college major would be philosophy (rather than chemistry or biology) and had signed up for an additional philosophy course.

My philosophy major lasted less than a year, however. The more time I spent in lectures and reading about philosophy, the more I became convinced of two things: (1) each writer's philosophical system seemed workable and incontestable if his premises were correct and (2) each writer's premises were in significant part based on assumptions rather than proof. My perception, right or wrong, was that the philosophers I was studying in college were thus guilty of jumping to conclusions.

The decision I then reached, therefore, was that I did not want to continue studying the philosophies of various thinkers if each of them made one or more assumptions and then built a system on that base, to explain time, life and death, the existence or nonexistence of God, a theory of knowledge, etc. Though this analysis of mine was probably superficial and wrongheaded, I figured I could make my own assumptions and do my own philosophizing.

The concept of time makes more sense to me, as it does to many other people, if time is viewed as circular rather than linear. For me, this eliminates concerns about beginnings and endings and about an answer to that old question: If God created the world, who created God? I don't believe I would be convinced by an argument that those concerns are also eliminated if linear time is viewed as extending infinitely in both directions. Perhaps my view of time is a reason why one of the few things I liked in Hermann Hesse's *Siddhartha*, when I got around to reading it, was the passage where Siddhartha says to Govinda, "I am not going anywhere. I am only on the way."

My principal concern as to postdeath experience is not the possibility of suffering the torments of hell (which I think is no possibility at all, for anyone) but the possibility that I will lose my identity. This could occur for any one of several reasons, including (1) one's consciousness being absorbed into God upon death, (2) death being followed by nothing but oblivion, and (3) one's consciousness becoming associated, upon death, with another identity. My concern about losing my identity is obviously a predeath concern. If it happens, there will be no "I" to be aware of or care about the loss after "I" cross the bar.

That death will result in the loss of one's identity is suggested by the virtually limitless variety of identities (and, hence, memories) amongst humankind, each individual's identity apparently being unique. It is very difficult to conceive (let alone accept) the postdeath existence of a consciousness whose only identity is a person who lived for five minutes or a person who died of starvation at the age of two or a person who was Adolf Hitler. The only way in which the survival of such identities is conceivable to me would be in the context of reincarnation, for reincarnation seems consistent with either the loss or the preservation of prior identities. One's consciousness becoming associated with another identity upon death need not involve a loss of the prior identity. There could be an awareness of prior identities in a between-times period, so to speak. And during one's lifetime, there could also be awareness of prior identities in Bridey Murphy–type situations, dreams, hypnotic trances, etc.

It is also conceivable to me that each of us could instead get on the wheel of time at the same spot again and give it another shot. It could be that you do go around more than once. I also recognize that the answer could be something that I (and, perhaps, all of us) cannot conceive.

As concerns the possibility of life existing on planets other than earth, I have no fixed opinion other than the one most of us no doubt have—it's possible. Naturally, I've seen a great deal in various media concerning possible alien visitations. In addition, I've seen documentaries on television regarding possible sightings of angels. Something I find strange is that the two subjects seem to be treated as mutually exclusive—that is, when aliens are the subject of discussion, no mention is made of a possibility that what might actually be involved is angels, and vice versa.

With respect to why God would permit all of the evil, misery, and suffering that exists in the world, the best explanation I've heard was given by a preacher in a Sunday sermon many years ago. He pointed out that there would be no merit in us if everything were, in effect, presented to us on a silver platter; and he suggested that it is only through working, struggling, persevering, and enduring that we become worthwhile human beings.

Of much more importance than pondering and speculating about metaphysical subjects, it seems to me, is figuring out how best to live the lifetime that each of us, with absolute certainty, is now aware of. Unfortunately, the prospect of death is something that is faced pretty much throughout that lifetime, and determining how to deal with that prospect is part of our task. When I was young, I often tended to be preoccupied with thoughts of death. Later it became evident to me that we should seek to avoid worrying about the prospect of death, at least until death comes.

We should also concentrate on the fact that our age right now is the youngest each of us is going to be and that right now each of us has as long to live as we ever had—an indefinite time. As in the case of any of my ideas, I am surely not the first person to come up with the thoughts that I have expressed. For example, in a book I read long ago, there was a reference to the Zen saying "Talk when you talk, walk when you walk, and die when you die." Similarly, in answer to Boswell's question "But is not the fear of death natural to man?" Samuel Johnson is said to have replied, "So much so, Sir, that the whole of life is but keeping away the thoughts of it."

In an earlier chapter, I endorsed the idea that we should concentrate on how good we are being to the other guy, not on how bad the other guy is being to us. It's easy enough to express this idea but not so easy to live up to it. The effort to concentrate on your own conduct instead of the conduct of others may be aided if you remember that your view of and reaction to a situation may depend upon your perspective. Today you may be a pedestrian who has the right-of-way in a crosswalk and is inclined to resent a driver who seems to be seeking to intimidate you into yielding that right-of-way. But tomorrow you may be a driver who is turning a corner and is inclined to resent a pedestrian who seems to be taking his own sweet time to cross the street.

At some point it became apparent to me that our main goal should be not to achieve happiness for ourselves but, instead, to create happiness for others. Once again, an idea easy to express but perhaps not so easy to carry out. We can only try.

Chapter 31

Strange Things

Unexpected Destinations

The kinds of strange things I am denoting by the above subhead are things that, I feel sure, we all encounter—namely, the strange or unusual places where objects sometimes land or arrive after being thrown, dropped, flipped, tossed, etc., at a particular target for the first time or, perhaps, at no target. The arrival of the object at the unexpected destination will usually elicit from me some such spoken or unspoken reaction as, "I couldn't do that again if I tried thousands of times."

For example, way back when I was in college, I threw a beer can at a metal wastebasket as hard as I could, for the first time in my life. Instead of going into the wastebasket, the beer can hit the rim and bounced back and clipped me right on the bridge of my nose, leaving a small cut. Probably because of the result of this first throw, I have never again thrown a beer can at a wastebasket as hard as I can.

I expect we all throw, drop, flip, toss, etc., lots of different objects at wastebaskets and other targets—everything from wadded-up paper, wrappings, cans, and plastic containers to snowballs. In our household, because we have a number of cats, Nancy and I also throw around a lot of balls, catnip bags, and other cat toys in the course of playing with our pets. I can't begin to remember all of the unexpected destinations reached by objects that I have thrown, dropped, flipped, tossed, etc., over the years. And I wouldn't attempt to describe them if I could, for in most cases it seems to me that an unexpected destination is something that needs to be seen to be appreciated and that is very difficult to adequately describe in words.

Nevertheless, one other incident will be mentioned, inasmuch as it made me conscious of the unexpected destination phenomenon—that something done perhaps once in a lifetime may have an absolutely astounding result. Years ago when the kids were young, I was clearing various items out of the sandbox located five or six feet from the back stoop of our house and picked up a spoon and flipped it toward the stoop, with the intention of taking the spoon into the house when I completed my sandbox project. This was, not surprisingly, the only time in my life I had flipped or tossed a spoon toward the back stoop or, indeed, anywhere else. In any event, the spoon clattered through the metal railing at the side of the stoop, bounced on the stoop a couple of times, and then came to rest with the bowl of the spoon balanced on the edge of the stoop and the handle projecting over the edge.

In case you are wondering why I have not mentioned my golf game in connection with the matter of unexpected destinations, I want to point out the difference between unexpected destinations and undesired destinations. Although the destinations of almost all of my golf shots were undesired, I can't say that those destinations were unexpected. That, in a nutshell, summarizes the problem with my golf game.

Attraction and Repellence

It is my understanding that there are persons who are allergic to the stings of certain insects and, if stung, will be in very big trouble unless prompt medical attention is made available.

I appear to be the opposite of such persons, for I seem to repel stinging insects. This was demonstrated in the yard at the house that Barbara and I first owned. It contained several fruit trees, including one pear tree. Every autumn overripe pears would fall on the ground and start to rot. This attracted scads of bees. In my efforts to pick up and dispose of these ripe, overripe, or rotting pears, I had to compete with the bees, who wanted the pears for their own purposes. This made it necessary for me to reach in amongst the squadrons of bees who were on the pears, on the ground near the pears, or hovering above the pears. I was never stung.

The only time I ever was stung by a bee occurred when I was at a picnic and took off my shoes for a while for some reason I don't recall. During the time when I was shoeless, a bee evidently crawled into one of my shoes; so when I subsequently put my shoes on again, I got stung. I couldn't really blame the bee, for he pretty much had no choice but to sting my foot.

In another incident I will describe, I was not stung and was damn glad of it. The house where we lived at the time had grooved vertical siding and a wooden molding where the siding met the bottom of the eaves. On the day in question, I was painting this molding and the underside of the roof overhang, when I was reminded that I had previously, from time to time, seen wasps crawling into openings created where a groove in the siding met the molding.

The reminder was a wasp coming *out* of such an opening, flying right into my cheek, not stinging me, bouncing off, and continuing on its merry way. Luckily I wasn't so startled as to lose my balance and fall to the concrete at ground level below me. The chance of this happening would, I suppose, have been much greater if I had been stung. Afterwards, I realized that the smell of nearby paint may have induced the wasp to take flight.

The Speeds of Light and Sound

As most everybody knows, light travels at a much, much greater speed than sound. Most of us have seen demonstrations of this at fireworks displays, where we see the flash before we hear the explosion. I had a somewhat different slant on this when I lived in a house a half mile or so from the high school football field. I was listening to a game on the radio one night when the festivities at the field included some fireworks at halftime. In this case I didn't see flashes at all but would hear an explosion on the radio broadcast and then, a second or two later, hear the same explosion again.

On one evening long ago, I had an encounter, at very close quarters, with the difference in speed between sound and light. Nancy and I had been conversing while I was in one of the rooms upstairs and she was in an adjacent room. As I was stepping out of the room where I had been, I wondered whether Nancy was still upstairs and glanced toward the adjacent room. I saw that the room was dark and concluded that Nancy had gone downstairs. An instant later I heard the click of the light switch in the adjacent room and saw Nancy step out of the darkened room. Even at a distance of only three feet or so, the different speeds of light and sound seem to have created in me a sequence of perceptions rather than a single perception. This incident also seems to say something about the speed at which impulses travel through the human nervous system to and from the brain.

Premonitions and Dreams

During a period of time a number of years ago, something that crossed my mind from time to time during waking hours was the possibility of having a blowout while driving on an expressway. Each time I had such a thought, I immediately rejected it, for I had had a blowout on an expressway about twenty-five years previously. And surely, I told myself, there would not be two expressway blowouts in one lifetime.

It may be that I didn't check my tire pressures as frequently as I should, and probably the same is true as to rotating my tires. With an old car having tires purchased on rather widely different dates, it might be hard to decide which tire ought to go where in the rotation procedure. In addition, I didn't keep track of the date or mileage when I bought any of the tires. But I thought that none of this was of significance—I had already experienced my expressway blowout.

You know where I'm going, so I might as well acknowledge that I did have another blowout on a freeway. About an hour before this happened, I had walked around the car and looked at all four tires. They looked okay to me, but what do I know? My blowout occurred when I was on my way home from visiting Warren at the retirement home. On the way out to see Warren earlier that day, I had stopped at a store to buy a couple of things, including the *Chicago Sun-Times.* I noticed at the time that the front-page headline on the newspaper read, "Tire tread blowouts killing without notice." "No problem," I thought. I'd already had my blowout on the freeway.

When it comes to dreams, I expect yours are about as strange as mine. Also, like me, you may have difficulty remembering just how strange your dreams are because at the moment you wake up on most mornings, you forget most or all of the details of the night's dreams, if any. One dream I had when I was twenty years of age I did remember very well the next morning…and ever since. It foretold the end of my engagement to a young lady I will refer to as Amy Lowder.

In that dream I went to see Amy and found that another young man was present and that Amy was ending her relationship with me. I believe it was the very next day when I received a letter from Amy breaking our engagement. I recognize that Amy could take the position that our engagement had been only a qualified one, for the next thing she said after expressing a desire to marry me was an inquiry as to whether I would convert to Catholicism, to which I made a noncommittal response.

My nocturnal premonition about the end of our engagement was no stranger than the engagement itself. No, I'm not referring to how strange it was that any young lady would accept my proposal but, rather, to the fact that we never saw one another after the night I proposed and she accepted. The next day after our engagement, I returned to college in New England. I received Amy's letter before the end of the college semester and my return to Illinois. Although I made one futile telephone call to her after receiving her letter, and there was a little further correspondence back and forth later, we never saw one another again.

Another aspect of dreaming that I consider strange is my awareness—sometimes—that I'm dreaming. This awareness usually takes the form of some such impression as, "Boy, I'd sure be concerned or frightened about this situation I'm in if I didn't know I was dreaming." My dreams often involve me in chase situations, where, either alone or as part of a group, I am being chased by others or I am chasing others. In a dream somewhere along the line, I caught up with those whom I was chasing and was convinced by them that they were the good guys after all. This is the only dream I can remember where I changed sides.

For a number of my adult years, I had a more scary type of recurrent dream. It involved a specific house located very near to the school where I spent most of my grade school years. I was never in the house and probably walked past it very few times during my childhood (not because I was afraid of it but because it was located on the other side of the school from the neighborhood where I lived). During much of my adult life I drove past this house fairly often, but in my waking hours the house was never a source of fear or any other emotion.

In my dream I was afraid of the house because I thought there was something unknown and terrible inside. I was drawn to the house out of curiosity and because someone was seeking to persuade me to go inside, but I was afraid to enter. Over a period of months, or perhaps even years, the dream progressed to the point where I entered the house, looked through various rooms, found nothing terrible, and realized that the unknown and terrible thing must be in the basement. (Believe it or not, as I wrote the first draft of this paragraph, chills went up and down my spine several times.) The dream then moved to the next stage, where I went into the house, the unidentified someone tried to persuade me to go down to the basement, and I resisted. There were a number of times when I would look at the stairs leading to the basement but would not go down. I didn't want to find out what was in that basement. At last, however, a night came when I went down to the basement and found…nothing. In my dream I looked all through the basement and found the usual basement-type things but nothing terrible.

Thus ended my series of recurrent scary dreams about that innocent old house. Once I went down into the basement and found nothing fearsome there, I never again had a frightening dream about the house. However, there was an aftermath sometime later when I dreamed that I described to someone the dreams I used to have about the house.

The Moving Furniture Covers

During the wintertime the porch furniture that Nancy and I had out on the deck in front of our Chicago townhouse was covered with some plastic furniture covers. When warm weather came, we stored these covers on the bottom level of some metal shelving in our garage.

One summer day I noticed that these covers were no longer entirely on the bottom shelf but, instead, had overlapped in part onto the garage floor. When I reached down and pushed the plastic covers back onto the shelf, I felt some teeth on my hand for an instant and then heard the sound of an animal scuttling away. Although I never saw the perp, it was obvious that I had managed to allow myself to be bitten by a rat.

I tell myself that when you see something out of place, it is a natural reaction to put it back where it belongs. However, I also have to admit that I should have realized that plastic furniture covers don't take it upon themselves to get a little exercise, by sliding from a bottom shelf onto the floor or otherwise. Anyone with half a brain would have known that some animal must have nested within the plastic covers, at least temporarily; that part of the covers had flopped onto the garage floor because such animal had moved around in its "nest" in the process of making itself comfortable; and that such animal could be in this "nest" at the very time when I arrived at the garage. And in our Chicago neighborhood, "such animal" was bound to be Brer Rat.

Luckily for me, our rats ran small and had small teeth, so the momentary bite didn't break the skin. Though I was none the worse for wear by reason of my rat bite, I was, of course, somewhat the worse for embarrassment. Here again we would have a candidate for my stupidest moment, but for the fact that I had walked in front of Sonny at the edge of the dump in days of yore.

Antique Antics

Years ago I got into a problem with a suburban antique shop where I happened to use a credit card to pay for a $15 purchase. Later on the same day, I received a telephone call from the shopkeeper, who told me that part of my credit card number did not come through on the slip and asked me to give him the entire number so that he could write in the balance of the number. A couple of days later the shopkeeper called again, to advise that the bank would not honor a credit card slip bearing a partially handwritten card number (no surprise) and to request that I send him a check. I said that I would do so if he would first send me the credit card slip that I had signed. Two or three days later I received yet another call, and this time he complained that he had sent me the credit card slip but hadn't received a check from me. I told him I had just received the slip, that my practice was to pay bills each weekend, and that his bill would be one of those I would pay on the following weekend.

That was the end of the telephone calls, but before the weekend arrived, I received a form dunning letter from a lawyer stating that he represented the antique shop in connection with its $15 claim against me and that, if I didn't make payment immediately, I would be sued for the $15, plus attorneys' fees, etc., etc. I thought this whole scenario was pretty funny and described it to Chub Dawson and some of the other guys at the office. Chub offered to represent me and claimed that he could probably settle the matter for $7.50.

However, I decided instead to write a letter responding to the lawyer's dunning letter. I had previously had business dealings with one of the other lawyers at the same law firm; so I wrote him a letter, enclosed my check for $15 and a copy of the letter I had received from his colleague, and complained about his firm's debt collection procedures, particularly the issuance of a dunning letter within a matter of days after I had been billed and the improper assertion of a claim for attorney's fees. A short time later I received a letter of apology.

After All These Years

A while back, I helped out one of the other lawyers in the firm where I worked, in connection with a client's acquisition of a company located in Florida. In the course of this, I became aware that the president of the Florida company was a fellow that I'll call Bill Thedrakis. I remembered that when I was a little kid back home there was a slightly older kid with that name who lived in the neighborhood for a while and then moved away. A little later I had occasion to talk to Mr. Thedrakis about the current transaction and inquired as to whether he was that other kid. He acknowledged that he was and that he had moved away from the neighborhood about fifty years earlier, and he also mentioned that he had no recollection of me whatsoever.

My first reaction to this small world incident was a desire to mention it to some of the other guys from the old cemetery days. But then it occurred to me that I hadn't seen or talked to any of them for forty years or more. I managed to restrain myself from trying to get in touch with someone I hadn't seen in forty years to tell him I had spoken to someone else neither of us had seen in fifty years.

Chapter 32

The Strangest Thing

The incidents to be described in this chapter are more than mere strange things, and either may qualify as the strangest thing.

Candidate No. 1.: *The burned-out lightbulbs.* This happening has to do with the way we become aware that a lightbulb has burned out—namely, we turn or flip the switch and the bulb flashes for an instant and then goes out. The scene was a winter morning at the three-level apartment where Nancy and I lived a number of years ago, and the occasion was my customary morning trip from our bedroom upstairs to the bathroom in the basement, for purposes of shaving, etc. (I shaved in the basement bathroom because the medicine cabinet in the bathroom upstairs didn't have shelf space sufficient to hold both Nancy's stuff and my stuff.)

Upon leaving the bedroom, I flipped the switch in the upstairs hall in order to turn on the hall light. The bulb flashed and went out. I carefully made my way downstairs in the darkness and flipped the switch at the foot of the stairs to turn on the light located there. Again, there was a flash and this light also went out. Still in darkness, I groped my way to the head of the basement stairs and again flipped a wall switch. Eureka! The light in the basement at the foot of the stairs went on and stayed on. I walked down the stairs, went into the bathroom, and flipped the light switch. The light above the bathroom basin flashed and went out.

Three lightbulbs had burned out at virtually the same time. Yes, one other light that I had turned on did stay on, but that just demonstrates that the flashing and burning out of the other bulbs was not due to a house-wide or neighborhood-wide electrical problem. The replacement bulbs that

I put in the three lights worked fine; the three bulbs that burned out had not been installed at the same time; and the usage of the three lights was, of course, by no means identical.

It seems to me that three unrelated lightbulbs in one apartment burning out in a matter of seconds must be something like a million-to-one shot and could well be the strangest thing.

Candidate No. 2.: *The well-balanced paper clip.* Some years after the incident just described, this candidate for the strangest thing occurred while I was sitting at my desk in the law office where I worked.

As I recall, I was holding an envelope containing various office-type items, including paper clips, and for some reason I don't recall, I slowly emptied the contents of the envelope onto the desk. One of the common size paper clips landed on the desk on its side and stayed standing on its side (i.e., it did not fall over). I did not photograph the paper clip, for this was prior to the era of cell phone cameras.

I searched for a reason to explain how this could have happened. There was no evidence of paste or glue on the desk onto which the paper clip had fallen, no source of magnetism, and no narrow groove in the wooden top of the desk into which the clip had fallen. Perhaps an angel had caught and held the paper clip.

I sat there, pretty much transfixed for a minute or so, then picked up the paper clip and unsuccessfully tried to replace it in the same position. Perhaps the angel had released the paper clip as I picked it up.

In any event, it seems that this event is well qualified to be regarded as the strangest thing.

Chapter 33

My Redeeming Social Value

You may have noticed that the preceding pages have been, to a large extent, a farrago of my failings, follies, frailties, failures, foibles, and other folderol and foofaraw. It's time I made it clear that I am nevertheless a worthy and meritorious person. As a matter of fact, my old law partner Chub Dawson used to say to me, "Gabler, you're perfect." All right, I suppose I shouldn't quote Chub out of context and should instead tell you all of what he said—viz., "Gabler, you're perfect. A perfect asshole."

I suppose it has become obvious to everyone, including me, that Chub's comment (whether or not he was joking) will not tend to establish what I'm seeking to establish here. Accordingly, in order to demonstrate my redeeming social value, I think I'll cite some of my good qualities and describe some incidents that confirm my possession of those attributes.

Physically, I am in reasonably good shape for a man of my age and "achievements." I have so far managed to avoid becoming bald. Good news concerning the hair I now have is that some of it is still black. The bad news is that the black hair is located in my ears or other unsavory sites. As to my weight, there was a period during my adulthood when I was apparently somewhat overweight. However, I subsequently slimmed down again and without resorting to one of those weight-loss salons like Tubby or Not Tubby.

I recognize that if I'm to establish my redeeming social value, it will have to be on the basis of traits other than my hair and my weight. In this connection I can mention that I am accommodating and helpful to my friends.

For instance, early one evening during my senior year in college, I was hard at work in the library when Don, my high school and college classmate, joined me and suggested that we go into town and catch a movie. I resisted and he persuaded, and this process went on for a time. Ultimately, I gave in to his suggestion that we go down to the other end of the reading room, where the newspapers were kept, and check out what flicks were playing downtown. I spotted one that I would be willing to see but Don decided that there was nothing he was interested in. So I went alone. Not only did I give in to Don's entreaties, but I went so far as to carry out his original movie objective—all by myself.

Prior to the final examination in one of my law school courses, two of my classmates, Clem and Charlie, got together with me a couple of times to review the course and prepare for the exam. (I did this even though on another occasion, when Clem had called the apartment where my wife and I lived, Charlie grabbed the phone away from Clem and in a loud voice said, "Gabler eats shit." Charlie was quite embarrassed when he learned, moments later, that Clem had been talking to Barbara rather than me.) In any case, while the three of us were preparing for that final examination, I got the impression that Clem and Charlie just didn't understand a number of the concepts involved in the course. I therefore went out of my way to explain one point after another to them. I was so helpful to them that they each got an A on the final exam, Clem's grade on the exam being the highest in the entire class. Me? I got a B.

In addition to bending over backwards for my friends, I am courteous to total strangers. I will inflict on you only one example of this trait. During our daughter Pat's college days, Barbara and I took her to O'Hare airport to put her on a plane back to school one spring day. I dropped them off at the terminal and parked the car in a small lot which at that time was adjacent to this particular terminal. When I joined Barbara and Pat, I told them that something interesting had happened in the parking lot, involving a big black fellow I had encountered there. An African American woman happened to be in line right behind my family members, and Barbara used body language to make me aware of this, evidently fearing that I might otherwise say something offensive.

I had already noticed that lady and went ahead with my description of the parking lot incident. On the way to the terminal I approached an opening in the fence around the parking lot and saw that this big black guy was approaching the same opening from the other direction. As it turned out, we both arrived at the same time and I waited to let him pass through first. As he did so, I said to him, "How are you doing, Mr. Van Lier." His response was, "I'm tired." The lady standing next in line after Barbara and Pat shared their excitement about my having just conversed with a Chicago Bulls player.

Just one other desirable attribute of mine will be noted: I cook a mean hamburger. Once when Nancy's friend Stuart Padydyat was over at our place for a hamburger dinner, I asked him how many hamburgers he would like. His response was, "Is there a limit?" Would you believe that Stuart's friends called him Stu?

There was another time when I was cooking hamburgers for Nancy and me on our grill in the breezeway, while a big party hosted by one of our neighbors had partygoers thronging in the courtyard to which the breezeway led. When I went out to check on our last hamburger, I found no hamburger and realized that one of the party guests had picked it up off the grill and walked (or ran) off with it. Although these episodes give you an idea of the popularity of my hamburgers, honesty requires that I admit that the real attraction is Nancy's seasoning, not my cookery.

In any event, I also recognize how ridiculous this exercise has become. Here I am, apparently seeking to establish my redeeming social value by my alleged skill in cooking hamburgers. I think now it would be better to forget the whole idea of endeavoring to prove my merit and just tell you two things:

1. Rod named one of his daughters Paula, and
2. Georgia named one of her sons Paul,

and let it go at that.

Appendix A

Photographs

1. Paul in 2015 with Sophie, his favorite pet ever.
2. Rod playing Blockhead with four of Paul's children several decades ago.
3. One of Paul's annual readings of *The Night Before Christmas* to the children.
4. Georgia's "tea party" many years ago, for a couple of her dollies and special guest Paul.
5. Uncle Howard holding fat baby Paul, many, many years ago, with Rod looking on and the old cemetery in the background beyond the fence.

1. Paul in 2015 with Sophie, his favorite pet ever.

2. Rod playing Blockhead with four of Paul's children several decades ago.

3. One of Paul's annual readings of *The Night Before Christmas* to the children.

4. Georgia's "tea party" many years ago, for a couple of her dollies and special guest Paul.

5. Uncle Howard holding fat baby Paul, many, many years ago, with Rod looking on and the Old Cemetery in the background beyond the fence.

Appendix B

On the pronunciation of the letters "ch" at the beginning of words in the English language

Re: The "Chindig"

Hope you are planning to attend the above, which will be held at a suburban chateau or, if that's not available, at a nearby chalet. Everyone is invited—except there may be some feeling of chagrin if any charlatans with chancres show up.

Dinner will include chinook salmon and chiffon cake prepared by the chef, and after dinner cheroots will be supplied.

It will be more fun than a charivari, and the champagne will really flow (but try to restrain yourself from swinging on the chandeliers).

The entertainment will consist of charades and the singing of chanteys by a well-known chanteuse. Come with an escort if you wish, and if you like the military type come with that chivalrous chevalier with all his chevrons. Or come alone if you feel chauvinistic. In any event chaperons will be supplied.

Wear what you like. If you feel daring, wear that chartreuse chemise that's in your chiffonier. Put your hair up in a chignon and be chic in your chapeau.

Transportation is also optional. Use a chamois to shine your Chevrolet chassis, and hire a chauffeur to drive you over. Or come in a chaise or, if you want, arrive by chute.

If you feel that the above has involved some chicanery, let me nevertheless leave you with one thought: In the future when you discuss pronunciation, keep in mind where you are—at least when you are in Chicago!

Appendix C

A Tale of Two Kitties

Copyright © 2015 by Nancy W. Gabler

Little did I know that by checking out a new, local pet store in our Lincoln Park neighborhood one weekday afternoon our lives would change from that day forward. Not in a huge way, but in a significant way. As I have often found, by attending a new local store opening, they usually have opening day specials, and, because I was always looking for bargains/sales regarding pet food, accessories, etc., I decided I would see what was being offered that particular day.

The store was small and compact—a ground floor plus a basement. As I drifted toward the basement stairs, I saw a sign that read: "Live Animals Downstairs." Immediately a couple of red flags appeared in my mind. One reason I don't go to shelters in general—the Humane Society, Anti-Cruelty, etc.—is that I fall in love too easily. I would look at those cages and have my heart broken over and over again. Every cat I had ever acquired in my life, with the exception of two being gifts from coworkers, was a stray that I literally picked up off the street. So I hesitated—and then continued down the stairs.

Most of the basement area was devoted to cats—cat food, litter boxes, cat toys—a veritable array of anything feline. There was also a small section devoted to small animals. I made a point of looking around carefully, noting the opposite corner of the room containing the cages. Eventually, the "magnet" of the cages drew me over.

The black and white kitten was the perfect tuxedo. Perfection in the tuxedo world of black and white cats, from what I've seen in cat shows and read in books, consists of a fairly uniform color pattern: black back and back of head, white underside and legs, and the face—ahhh, the face—black mask that fans out over the eyes and upper cheeks and then the white pyramid that rises up the lower cheeks with the tip rising to just beyond the upper nose area. Looking like all of that and more, the kitten peered forlornly out of this big cage that threatened to swallow it up, anxiously watching clerks and customers passing it by. I walked over to the cage and its eyes rested on me. We stood gazing at each other for a few moments when a salesclerk approached me. "Would you like to see him?" I thought to myself, "Him?" "He" seemed like a "her"; the smallish eight-month-old kitten just seemed feminine. Dismissing that for the moment, I said, "Oh... Okay." "He" was put into my arms, and I think at that moment... you guessed it—I *did* fall in love, although I was trying to ignore it. "He" made a few squeaky sounds while the clerk directed me over to a table where I set the kitten down and proceeded to play with it with the help of some toys. "He" got very excited over the attention while the salesclerk was telling me how they all had had fun playing with "this one."

In the kitten's excitement, she/he nipped me in the thumb while grabbing at the toy I was holding. The clerk stopped in midsentence and hurriedly walked over to a fellow employee across the way. I looked at my thumb—a little nick, a tiny bit of blood—and then glanced over at the clerks, wondering what all the fuss was. I petted the kitten and she/he continued to play, pouncing on the "prey." I then kind of froze when I overheard one of them say one word: "unadoptable."

From my experiences with walking marathons for shelters and doing volunteer work for various no-kill shelters, I know what that word signifies for kill shelters: If the animal is deemed unadoptable, it generally is put down—in other words, put to sleep. I looked at this lovely, sweet kitten playing happily, and, before I even realized I was speaking, I said to the clerks, "I'll take the cat." They both turned and studied me for a moment, then slowly approached me. "But the kitten *bit* you." "Don't be silly, it was just an accident. It's a lovely kitten—I'll take it. Write it up." One clerk shrugged and looked at the other, who had a similar response. The clerks explained to me that I would have to sign some sort of waiver, for liability reasons, and I assured them that was no problem.

As I stood waiting for them to get a cardboard carrier to transport the kitten in, I looked at the now-empty cage and noticed a little white sign taped in the corner of the cage. The sign read, "I come with Sweetie." I sighed, thinking, "What could *that* possibly mean? Who's Sweetie?" When I spotted one of the clerks again, I asked her about the sign. "Oh," she said, "'he' had a sister and they slept curled up with each other all the time." As she disappeared to finish preparing the kitten to accompany me home, I thought, "Huh…there was another one." After they presented the kitten to me in the carrier, I asked the clerk again, "Soooo, what happened to Sweetie?" "Oh, she was sent back to the Anti-Cruelty Society because she got sick." I stood there for a few seconds, absorbing that, thinking, "Oh, my God, 'he' has a sibling, who 'he' was no doubt missing, which is why 'he' looked so forlorn in that cage." Again, I quizzed her. "So, what do they do? Do they cure the cat and then put the cat up for adoption again?" I was a little afraid of the answer, with good reason. "Well," she said, "as far as I know, sometimes they try to cure, *but*, if they're really crowded, sometimes the cat is just put down." "But," she went on brightly, "'she' wasn't all *that* sick! However, we can't sell even slightly sick animals."

As the paperwork was prepared, I took the kitten out of the carrier to check her/him out and make sure everything was okay. I examined the kitten closely and found that my hunch was right—she was indeed a *girl*! When the clerk came back, I said, "I've got a bulletin for you—this kitten is a *girl*." "Oh," she laughed, "oops, a mix-up." Then I thought to myself, "What kind of place is this? They can't get their records straight, then they laugh it off?!" I wondered how long this pet store would last. (As it turns out, for one reason or another, this particular pet store only survived in the neighborhood for about five years.)

I pondered quite a few things on the way home: How was poor Sweetie doing? Could my new kitten's sibling be another girl? or possibly a brother? How badly was my kitten missing her sibling? Et cetera, et cetera.

My husband, Paul, was not happy that I brought another cat into our already multicat household, but he was soon charmed by our new kitten, who seemed to fit in nicely with her new roommates. But Sweetie haunted me. Sometimes I would see the new kitten, which by this time I had named Mandy, sitting alone or in a corner, very quiet, cleaning herself. I wondered if her sibling was doing the same thing, only in a very small cage.

The more I thought about Sweetie, the more I decided that fate put these cats in my path for a reason. I had a friend whose coworker was a volunteer at Anti-Cruelty. I asked my friend, Michelle, if she could possibly ask her coworker to get a tag number for me, explaining that a tuxedo cat was sent back to Anti-Cruelty on such and such a day from the new Lincoln Park pet store. Within a day I had a tag number.

I stared at that number and decided I needed to go to Anti-Cruelty and get that cat. It was a crazy idea, and I had a feeling Paul would be furious with me—again—as I hadn't even mentioned to him the possibility of acquiring yet *another* cat! But I looked at Mandy's little face and knew what my choice would be.

When I arrived at the big glass-walled building from the bus stop, I walked into Anti-Cruelty, kind of trembling with excitement, as I figured it would be a red-letter day for Mandy but maybe not such a red-letter day for me once my husband was aware I was bringing home another cat. "Well," I thought, "here goes nothing. Let's just see what fate has in store." All of that glass exterior contained windows for animal cages, so I remember murmuring to myself, "Don't look at cages, don't look at cages…"

I presented the tag number. The clerk disappeared and then came back with the pronouncement, "Well, the cat has a respiratory problem, but if you agree to pay for the meds, the cat is yours."

"That's it? Okay, done."

It all happened with stunning rapidity: I paid for the meds, the carrier was brought out, and I sat down in a chair in the waiting area and looked at the cat inside.

Not the perfect tuxedo! The cat was a good size, even *large*, actually, a bizarre zig-zaggy pattern on its sides where the black back met the underside white, and it had a kind of goofy face, *but*—those eyes. Big, round, concerned eyes that looked at me a bit anxiously.

This little lummox of a kitten was as imperfect as Mandy was perfect, but…you guessed it—I fell in love again!

"It's okay, Sweetie, you're going home now."

I became very concerned and wanted to reassure the cat, so I opened the carrier and lifted the cat out. Upon examination, *again*, my hunch was right. It was a boy cat, even though the documents said "female"—damn that pet store! Uneven, ragged markings along the sides—not the perfect symmetry of his sister's face—but a motorboat engine of a purr! I wrapped my arms around him and I thought to myself, "Okay, this is a *good* thing!" We sat like that for several minutes, with his front legs wrapped around my neck while I rocked in my seat. People passed back and forth in front of us in the waiting area, sometimes glancing at us and smiling.

As I put him back in the carrier, I looked at the accompanying papers and saw that the reason Anti-Cruelty had originally acquired him and his sister was that they "weren't wanted." Not wanted?? Well, somebody wanted them now.

When the cab dropped us off at home, I made my way into our house, our other cats looking up at me and the carrier curiously. I didn't see Mandy and wondered if she was off by herself, perhaps upstairs. I made my way upstairs and saw Mandy in the guest bedroom. We had an aquarium in that bedroom, and Mandy was sitting in front of it, watching the fish.

I gently closed the door behind me and put the carrier down on the floor.

"Mandy," I whispered. "Here's your brother!" She quickly jumped off the aquarium table and started to approach the carrier. I loosened the top and let the boy cat jump out.

When I have told this story to friends and family in the past, I always insert this comment: I have never seen a cat do a double take before! And that is precisely what happened: Mandy did a double take as this black and white cat, somewhat larger than her, leaped out of the carrier. To me, it was as if she'd said, "Wait! Is that my brother?!" Both of them, in unison, slightly raised their haunches, in a sort of self-defense mode, and their noses slightly wrinkled, but only momentarily. Within seconds, they literally rushed at each other and rubbed noses, the boy cat then rubbing his face against hers. Mandy made a few twiffling noises (for the uninformed, a twiffle is a cross between a meow and a purr) and proceeded to groom her brother's neck.

I stood there for a long time, alternately crying and laughing, and thought to myself, "I've done a *good* thing!" As I've often said in retelling this event, it's my best feline moment. Ever. They continued to inspect each other for several minutes, sometimes excitedly grooming each other, at other times just circling each other and checking out strange scents, trying to discover where the other had been. I stood there rooted to the spot, fascinated by the most remarkable reunion I have ever witnessed!

By the way, Paul was *not* happy with me at all, but he has grown to love "boy cat" and often calls him Pal, especially when boy cat sidles up to him to be petted.

We had a to-do concerning boy cat's name. At first we named him Elmo, but as soon as that name became somewhat official (at the vet's, for instance), it occurred to me that he seemed like the perfect Mooch, not only because of his penchant for butting other cats away from any food dish but also because I was fond of a comic strip named "Mutts" where the black and white cat, for the same reasons, was also named Mooch. So, for a while he was El Moocho, and then finally Mooch or Moochie settled in as his name.

For the record, Mandy and Mooch, to this day, are still best buds, still sleep intertwined with each other, and Mooch has certainly lived up to his original name, Sweetie. Whereas his sister is little miss tough girl, is basically very shy, gets "all riled up" after intense petting and "vents" by scratching on the Turbo Chaser, and still likes to nip sometimes, Moochie is as sweet as they come. They are more than twelve years old now, and Mooch is on medication for arthritis. Even though we administer two pills a day via a pill gun, he doesn't struggle or push us away with his front paws, as most cats will do. He comes up to my pillow in bed at night and purrs us both to sleep. When either of us walks into a room, even before Mooch is touched and/or petted, his little motorboat purr begins. He loves what Paul and I refer to as petting pods, where he has two or more people petting him at once—he happily parades around to each person in the pod to get his share of petting and then some. He is the most loyal, the most endearing male cat we have had—or perhaps will ever have.

Printed in the United States
By Bookmasters